My House of Lies

Awakening from a Childhood of Sexual Abuse

Lori Golden

My House of Lies
Awakening from a Childhood of Sexual Abuse

The incidents in this book appear essentially as I remember them;
however, the names and certain identifying features of some
people portrayed have been changed to protect their privacy.
Caution: descriptions of abuse are descriptive and vivid.

Book Consultant: Judith Briles, The Book Shepherd
Cover and interior design: Rebecca Finkel, F + P Graphic Design
Artwork: Lori Golden

Books may be purchased for educational and promotional use.
Please contact the author at
LoriGoldenAuthor@gmail.com

LCCN: 2019904171
ISBN (softcover): 978-0-9600267-0-8
ISBN (eBook): 978-0-9600267-1-5
ISBN (audiobook): 978-0-9600267-2-2

Child abuse | Sexual abuse | Self help

Little Lori ...

you did survive and

now we both thrive!

I dedicate this book to my son, Jason, who has been the greatest gift I have ever received.

To my sister, Karen, and my brother Peter who have lived in *My House of Lies*. The two people who have witnessed first hand my father's sexual abuse.

To my niece Tami and my nephew Michael for their support in my telling our family secret.

To Madelyn, my survivor buddy, who has heard every dirty secret I have carried, who was there in my worst and my best times and who continues to this day to be my loving supportive friend.

To Jamie, who has been my confidant since 1982 and has witnessed me in my addiction, in my recovery and who I have become today.

And to all survivors of sexual abuse.

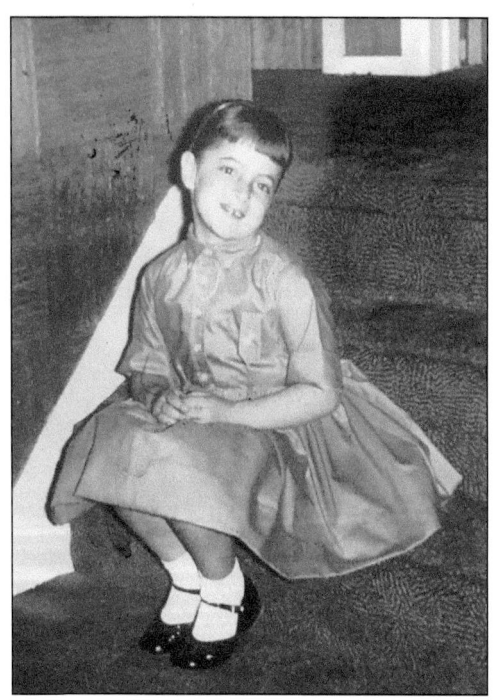

Lori, age 7

Contents

CHAPTER ONE

What is Happening to Me?

I thought I was going crazy.

NIGHT IS APPROACHING. My trapped feeling intensifies. Why did I feel so free during the day … yet at night, panic sets in?

I could no longer shower in the evening. My fear that an intruder would break in and I could not hear it happening haunted me.

When I showered, I was gripped by a creepy feeling of being watched. Repeatedly, I would pull the shower curtain aside to make sure no one was standing there. I kept visualizing the shower scene in the movie *Psycho*. When I finished, I would step out and then be afraid to open the bathroom door because someone could be standing right outside.

The idea that someone was going "to get me" grew stronger and felt real. It was as if I had lived this experience already.

The bedroom door was my barrier behind the bigger and stronger locks I had added to my apartment. Locks that I would check and recheck to make sure each locked properly. Noises and reverberations permeated the air. As I lay down, I'd listen for sounds of a possible intruder and think: *Maybe I need better locks on the door.*

Sleeping was difficult. My Valium intake was increasing as my sleeping pills were. I was easily startled and looked to my "pill friends" for relief.

When sleep came, the darkness began to feel evil. Shadows were envisioned as arms outstretched, coming to get me in the night. Nightlights were added to my rooms so I could see with more clarity as darkness invaded my space.

I thought I was going crazy. My shortness of breath, tightened muscles in my legs and shoulders, and listening acutely for sounds all highlighted my bizarre behavior. Nothing made sense.

I was a mature woman. I had such a good … such a perfect childhood. How could this—whatever "this" was—be happening to me?

CHAPTER TWO

New York, New York

Although Central Park was beautiful and provided a source of nature, it was not enough to quench my thirst—I needed more.

THE YEAR IS 1982. I am 32 and had just run the New York City Marathon, placing 795 out of 8,756 people. I trained hard, was disciplined and had accomplished my goal. At the same time, I was building my private practice after leaving my full-time job working at a mental health center. It was time to branch out on my own.

When I graduated with a master's degree in social work in 1978, I was determined to get a job at a mental health center where I would learn to do psychotherapy with clients. I was certain about my future. This was my goal since I went to therapy after having dropped out of college when I was 22 because of drug use. Clarity arrived when I stopped using drugs. I was meant to do therapy and help others. I had been there. I knew the extreme highs and lows.

After the marathon, a sciatic pain surfaced that emanated from my right hip down my leg. While swimming alleviated it and was something I learned at camp as a kid, swimming laps was something I had never done. I decided to work with a former Olympic swimmer to strengthen my skills. Again,

I was determined to achieve my goal and with my teacher's guidance, I did. I felt powerful gliding back and forth with ease through the water.

With my strength in swimming, scuba diving got my attention. Vacationing in the Bahamas, I became certified and immediately fell in love with diving. It was easy to be captivated by the depth of visibility; the 50 feet to the bottom were crystal clear. The richness of the coral reef was breathtaking. And watching the beautiful fish swim in and around the reef was mesmerizing. At that moment, I remembered how much I loved watching the fish in my father's fish tank. I always imagined that I was the little man in the tank blowing bubbles.

I felt the innocent wonderment of a child.

Scuba diving felt the way I always imagined it would if I were that man in the tank—so freeing, so unbelievably freeing. Here I could escape into a different world where I experienced the quiet of an underwater world. My thinking shut off and I heard the sound of my breathing in and out. Calmness pervaded my being. I let my guard down. I felt the innocent wonderment of a child. My awareness of wanting freedom grew. The question became: *freedom from what?*

It was indeed a weird sensation, but I felt I needed to run … to get away … to get out. *Why?*

Getting out of New York became my idea of achieving the ultimate freedom, away from the tall buildings and back to nature. I felt cooped up in my apartment, and there was a lot of dreary weather to contend with. I longed for bright sunlight and fresh air; elements not experienced in New York often enough.

Central Park was so beautiful and provided a source of nature, it was not enough to quench my thirst. I needed more.

Biking was added to my list of things I loved, and I quickly increased my routine to miles of lap-riding around Central Park. Like swimming, the movement of riding felt freeing as I challenged myself to go further and further in mileage.

At the time, I did not realize my need to exercise was fueled by a driving desperation. The same desperation drove me to swim and bike in order to settle down enough to be able to reside in my apartment. Yet I still felt trapped. I was constantly restless and did not know how to relax.

My aloneness and anxiousness were becoming more apparent.

Was I really unaware that I was using exercise bulimia and food addiction to get through the day … every day? Did I make a conscious decision not to acknowledge my body's telltale signs?

Occupied constantly with food thoughts, my mind became my enemy. I had a fear of getting *fat*—even though I was thin. I would count calories, binge and exercise, or simply not eat. I felt guilty and shameful if I ate too much. I also felt guilty if I did not want to exercise. And the constant need to push myself to do more was taking its toll on me.

My anxiousness was becoming more apparent. But I did not identify as having an eating disorder at this point. I was athletic and it made sense to maintain my "good body," which gave me a sense of self-worth. Inwardly I was constantly struggling with worthlessness. The outside world just did not see it … yet.

Work made me feel worthy, as did swimming, biking and maintaining a fit body. That was when I felt competent. As soon as I stopped doing those activities and quieted down, I felt worthless, alone, and trapped. My feeling of aloneness was intensifying. It felt dark and scary, so I made sure I was always doing an activity to keep it at bay. And my obsession about my being thin or fat on any given day, my obsession with food, calories and exercise served to keep my deeper self at arms-length.

Even though I was exercising regularly, it still did not calm my unexplained anxiousness. Sedatives and sleeping pills became my routine in the eighties. It was not until years later that I understood I was addicted to medications.

In 1984, a diving bliss trip was planned. I took off five weeks from my practice and flew to the Cayman Islands to earn my advanced certification. But sadly, during one dive, my eardrum was damaged, preventing me from doing something I loved for months. I felt a huge loss.

Anxiety and restlessness permeated me. Since I was not regularly working out, I became obsessive about my body. Here I was, in this amazing environment, and I was smoking weed, on Valium, and totally consumed with jealousy over a guy I was dating. My feeling of worthlessness along with increased feelings of aloneness and desperation were surfacing again. I could not stop my obsession with losing his attention. I was fearful that he would stop caring for me.

Why was my self-worth so dependent on a man's interest in me?

My drive to add more accomplishments continued. Next, I applied for a Cousteau trip. The destination was Mosquito Island with a group of people led by Jean Michelle Cousteau where underwater photography became an attraction. On that trip, I made a decision to move to a place where I could dive in beautiful water … and be warm. Plus, I longed to have the freedom that the water and warmth represented in my mind.

I felt if I stopped, I would die. I had to keep my body moving. I desired to be outside and away but had no clue what that actually meant. Enjoying the sunshine and outdoors seemed normal, but I was clueless as to why I had to keep getting away.

It was becoming clearer to me that something deep inside me was not right.

As a kid, I loved the summers and hated the winters, even though I loved to ski. I disliked the shorter days and the longer nights—I was stuck in my house. My yearning for open space and sunlight was growing as well as my avoidance of being indoors, dreading the transition from day to night. I came up with two options to my dilemma: Take a sedative or do a workout to calm down.

I didn't know why, but I did not trust my mother and often felt uneasy in her presence. When she called me to say that she was getting divorced—her second, I headed to San Diego to visit.

Another world unfolded in front of me in San Diego. I went scuba diving and fell in love with the environment, the climate, the availability to the ocean along with the nearby desert and mountains where snow skiing was possible in the winter. When I returned to New York, I made the decision to move to California.

It was becoming clearer to me that something deep inside me was not right. No amount of activity, work, friends, pills, food, medication and men made me feel okay. Where others saw me as successful, athletic, and a go-getter, I believed I was a fraud acting a part and pulling one over on everyone.

No one, including myself, could see that I was fueled by desperation. I could not stop. When I was alone in my apartment, I did not know what to do with myself. I could never concentrate on TV or read, something I had struggled with since second grade. My lack of reading at that time was shameful—I felt I was so stupid. My success with clients and with sports provided a shield for me to hide behind. The more accomplished I became, the more confusing my beliefs about myself felt and grew.

> It was getting harder and harder to stay on top of my growing belief that something was very wrong with me.

Nothing made sense. I would look in the mirror and see a reflection that I didn't recognize. *Who are you?* I would silently ask this stranger staring back at me. She felt unreal, confusing, filled with shame and I loathed her, but I did not know why. *Who am I?*

It was getting harder and harder to stay on top of my growing belief that something was very wrong with me. Focusing on this only created more confusion about myself, even though I had clarity when working with others. My strengths and my ability to work with people served to highlight that I was a mystery to myself.

I remember thinking if only I could see myself with the same clarity as I did for my clients, maybe I could figure out what was wrong with me. I yearned for something, but the yearning just grew, creating pent-up energy inside. My medication, exercise, and men provided only temporary relief. I did not yet see that my pill usage and my eating disorder were protecting me from the horror I had experienced as a child—protection from my inner truth.

Back in the '80s, the use of prescription pills was not a problem: The medical profession endorsed them. I never once questioned my usage of them or my terror at the thought of going off them. They were a part of my everyday life, and I always made sure an abundant supply was within arm's reach. My sleeping pill tucked me into bed at night, and Valium wrapped me in its soothing embrace to face the day when I woke. Each pill's support was needed in order to cope with the nighttime and then the daytime.

Indoor living was becoming intolerable and unsafe, but at the time, I did not understand why. I only knew I needed to get out. I kept asking myself, *out of what?*

I felt relief when I left my apartment. At times, I would run the stairs when it was too late to go out, or it was bad weather. I started on one side of the building, ran upstairs, and then ran down the hall to the opposite side where I would continue to the next floor. Alternatively, I ran to my pool club seeking to feel different from the way I did. I loved that it was an open space enclosed in large glass walls. The view was beautiful and overlooked New York. The indoor space was surrounded by an outdoor lounging area covered in fake grass and plants. I actually felt in nature and was comforted by the smell of the pool. As soon as the elevator doors opened into the club, I breathed a sigh of relief. I felt safe. I was around people. I could get out of myself in this environment and leave behind my growing dread of being alone and cooped up in my living space.

I also got out of myself when I wore my bathing suit. I was always aware of showing off my "good body" and receiving compliments from my family and friends. When men looked at my body, I felt in control and was shielded from my inside ugliness.

It became addictive.

My life was beginning to have a *Looking for Mr. Goodbar* edge to it. I had to be seen and have men's eyes on me. There were desperation and longing in just about everything I did in my personal life. My promiscuous behavior had no limits. I slept with younger lifeguards. Swimming and parading my body around in front of them became a fix for me but also a source of shame often thinking, *what is wrong with me, I am so sick.* Yet, even when I made a conscious decision to do so, I could not stop. I had to do what I did to feel self-worth.

I became good friends with people I slept with. The numbers grew *exponentially*—work colleagues, sports buddies, men who just admired my body, and ones I met through scuba diving. My body was available. At my surprise going-away party, my close friend Jamie invited all my male friends. We joked as we looked around the party and pointed to each person I slept with.

It felt like everyone else had love in his or her life but me. None of my accomplishments felt worthwhile without a man. Sleeping with different men felt like I was in control and had power, always denying my remorse and shame afterward. I had to have a man in my life. When I didn't, I felt symptoms of withdrawal, anxiety, difficulty concentrating on my activities, isolated, worthless and being unlovable. It did not matter how many friends I had or my connection to family.

Without a man, I was alone, and nothing filled this void. When I became conscious of this feeling, it was painful to live with. *Why did it dictate my self-worth?*

I remember looking at the book *I'm Dancing as Fast as I Can* about a woman addicted to Valium and her trying to live life without it. Of course, this was not me. After all, I was functioning well. I was not like her and I was not addicted. I could stop at any time; I just did not want to.

A few months prior to leaving New York, my apartment building complex went condominium, opening the window to purchase the rights to my apartment for a few thousand dollars and immediately turn around and sell it for $50,000. I was thrilled to have a safety net.

With a position in a group practice in San Diego offering me the same percentage split as my New York practice, I was packed and ready to go. I was determined to change my life around … once again.

The beauty of denial kept me isolated from myself. I was yearning for the truth while at the same time doing everything to keep me from it.

I believed wholeheartedly that moving to San Diego delivered the answer I was searching for—a new life where I could start over. It would be a life that got rid of the old and brought in the new. I could reinvent myself. I loved the warm weather; surely, I would feel better there. I could be outside whereas, in New York, I was forced to be inside. I believed I was running from the New York City environment, not myself. I was getting away from the bad weather—weather that must be the culprit of my dark moods. I felt free out in nature, yet like a caged animal inside my apartment.

I loved my work and helping those I worked with—it was hard to give up.

It was January of 1986. I was 36. All I could understand is that it was "crazy" to yearn for something and to be driven by desperation. But I was positive that San Diego would be a better place to live and work. Moving would be the solution. I was determined to change my life around.

My desire to leave superseded my mistrust of my mother. Yet, I believed that if she could leave New York, so could I. California, here I come!

CHAPTER THREE

San Diego ... A New Life that Wasn't

No matter what I did to dim the light.
I could not shield myself adequately.

I REMEMBER MY FIRST NIGHT. The furniture and clothes had not yet arrived, and I was sleeping on the floor in an empty room. And I cried. *What had I done? What had I given up?* My friends, my practice, my apartment, the pool club, familiarity with New York, knowing my way around, working out of my apartment and not needing a car. A lot.

That first night, I was frightened, but over the course of the next year, my nighttime fear of an intruder intensified. I heard sounds outside my door and felt panicky. I longed for the security guards protecting my apartment complex when I lived in New York. Suddenly, being without the guards felt scary. Quietly, I held my breath listening for an intruder. *How was it possible I felt safer in New York City than in San Diego?* Never did I imagine an intruder when I was in my former apartment.

Purchasing a car was a big undertaking, as was driving around town. I had not bought, owned or driven a car for some time. Being unfamiliar with the streets and navigating around town was overwhelming. It was very different in 1986. I did not have a GPS, and I had trouble reading maps. I remember pulling over at different times and breaking down crying. At those moments, I imagined how a rat must feel trying to find a way through a maze to get the reward. What was my reward? Along with being frustrated, impatient and annoyed at myself for giving up all that was familiar, I felt so vulnerable in my new environment.

I wasn't settling into my new life in San Diego as I had imagined I would. Everything was unfamiliar; even the beautiful sunny days was an adjustment. The sun was always out, and it was January! I was used to feeling pressure in New York on a sunny day to get outside of my apartment and make the most of the good weather. Now it was good weather every day.

My couch became my destination, exhausted from the simplest decisions.

When I wanted to stay inside, the internal pressure to go out left me irritable, restless and discontent. Then, when I did push myself out, the thought of *where do I go?* was overwhelming. Bike riding and swimming were easier for me in New York. I was used to Central Park and my pool club. Now I had to buy a bike rack to drive to a park and drive to a gym to swim. Which gym should I join; which park had good biking?

Everything seemed like a big decision, and I was not up to figuring it all out.

My couch became my destination. I was exhausted from the simplest decisions.

I was grateful for my weekdays that revolved around work. There I felt my competency and my strength. The group of people I worked with made me feel welcomed. Soon my schedule filled, and I was back to seeing clients regularly.

I worked in a lovely surrounding and loved going out into the beautiful weather after a full day of work. The *now-what's-next* thinking was not as daunting. In time, I joined a gym and began swimming regularly and found routes for bike riding. The beach was only a 15-minute drive away, which gave me access to racewalking along the water.

Workout needs intensified and the restlessness I felt cooped up in my New York apartment followed me to San Diego. Here I was in beautiful San Diego where I had access to all that I loved in nature and wonderful weather. Beautiful, windy, sunny days and chilly nights. My belief that the restlessness and inability to relax inside was due to the city environment in New York. Now, what was my excuse?

On the days that rained, I noticed myself gearing up for a downpour day, only to have the sun come out a few hours later. This annoyed me. I would get ready for a rainy day. My mood lowered out of habit after growing up on the East Coast. Then the sun would appear, pressuring me to go out. The fluctuation in the weather delivered chilly nights. Out of habit, I told myself that I was freezing. People would laugh when I used that word and soon, I gave it up. The reality was that there really was no more freezing cold days and nights, and after several months, I began to relax and appreciate.

I met some underwater photographers with whom I regularly dove. I went out every weekend on a friend's boat and soon had to buy a dry suit in order to dive. Since I am small, a wet suite did not cut it. The Pacific Ocean was the coldest water I had dove in but also clear and beautiful. I particularly loved the kelp beds. Scuba diving helped me to settle indoors on the weekends, since afterward I was sufficiently wiped out from the sun and water.

As night approached, my trapped feeling intensified. During the day I felt free, at night I felt panic. I noticed I was easily startled and looked to my increasing use of Valium for relief Showering at night ceased—I could not hear if an intruder were breaking in. I would be in the shower when I was gripped by a creepy feeling of being watched, often pulling the shower curtain aside to make sure no one was standing there. I kept visualizing the shower scene in the movie *Psycho*. I would get out of the shower and be afraid to open the bathroom door because someone could be standing right outside. The idea of someone going "to get me" grew stronger and felt real. *Had I experienced this before?*

> Darkness began to feel evil. I envisioned shadows as arms coming to get me in the night.

Falling asleep was becoming more difficult. My answer was to increase my sleeping pill intake. I even had the doctor's okay. Better locks were added to my apartment door; locks that had to be checked and rechecked to make sure they were properly locked. I would stare at my bedroom door and listen for sounds of the intruder that I knew lurked about.

My shortness of breath, tightened muscles in my legs and shoulders, listening acutely for sounds all highlighted my craziness. Nothing made sense. Darkness began to feel evil. I envisioned shadows as arms coming to get me in the night. Night lights were added throughout my apartment, so I could see with more clarity into the dark.

What was wrong with me? I was beginning to think I was crazy...since I had such a good childhood and a loving family.

Wanting relief became more and more apparent. I could not sit quietly. I was consumed with frantic energy pushing me to move and do more: exercise more, take more sedatives, have more food thoughts, work harder, plan more scuba diving outings, and obsessing about more men. If I could only push and push and keep on pushing, I would find the answer.

I felt myself running away as fast as I could. But from what? It's a feeling of insanity. I wondered am I going crazy? I kept asking myself,

> *What is wrong with me?*
>
> *Why am I so restless and discontent?*
>
> *How come I feel worse than I did in New York?*
>
> *Why isn't the beautiful weather, the water, the beach, boating, and scuba diving making me feel better?*

Instead, I felt surrounded by a blackening cloud. I knew I was desperate because now I did not have my New York excuses: it's the buildings, too much cement, not enough nature, bad weather, not enough outside living. What now? I had all that I said I wanted in my environment. I moved, followed my dreams, only to feel I was living a nightmare.

I'm aware I am running to my pills. The more I use them, the more I want to deny my need, the more I want to use them to cover what I know I don't want to know. Consumed with food thoughts throughout the day and night distracting me from the moment, from my desperation, quieting the frantic building inside of me. At times, I want to scream and scream and scream. Taking a sedative quiets the scream; taking a sedative enables me to sit throughout the day so I can concentrate; taking sleeping pills earlier and earlier than my normal bedtime to escape the nighttime terror that is building—waking up in the middle of the night, taking more to ease back into sleep once again.

It's becoming harder to pretend nothing is wrong.

One of my new norms was not knowing what to do with myself as soon as my workday ended. What I did know was that the transition from work to home was increasing my anxiety. The remedy was two-fold: pop a pill to quiet down and as soon as I got home; then exercise until I was physically exhausted through biking, swimming, or hitting the gym. Eventually, a rhythm would hit, and my panic would begin to subside.

When I moved, I began sensing a growing awareness that "something" is buried inside me. At the same time, "what is wrong with me" repeats in my head like a never-ending tempo. And, what is the something?

With my love of scuba-diving, becoming an assistant instructor served my competitor spirit. Preparing for the test, I practiced in the pool of my apartment building complex. One day I was geared up in mask, snorkel, and weights without my tank for air. I jumped in and sunk to the bottom and immediately was seized with panic. My thoughts scattered and I couldn't remember what to do. The weights were holding me down, but I couldn't compute this. Instead, I felt "held down" and unable to move.

Not knowing up from down, I pushed off the bottom to get away from whatever was gripping as I thought, I'm going to drown. Help was what I need, but no one around the pool knew I'm in trouble. Screaming for help in my head., I finally got hold of the panic and simply released my weight belt. Dropping the belt and rising to the surface, I climbed out telling myself that I must appear in control.

I always had to appear in control regardless of how I felt.

A man I was dating was in the Jacuzzi and yelled out, "Are you okay?"

As I laughed, I said, "Of course, why wouldn't I be?"

"I was thinking you were under longer than usual holding your breath. Then you popped up—I was just worried,"

Hiding behind appearance was everything to me, always appearing in control regardless of how I felt. I made sure I hid my inside turmoil. No one at work; no one I was dating; my family and my friends could see how much I was suffering— I made sure of it (at least, I thought I did). I did not have the words to go with it, nor did I understand the severity of it. If I looked good with nice clothes and a good figure, I believed I appeared in control.

Being a therapist went along with my being-in-control belief. My suffering was secondary to helping others. Helping others find relief from their inside pain was essential in my work— doing so allowed me to feel I was in my element when I was with clients. But outside of that, I was lost and spiraling out of control. I no longer made sense of myself. Maybe I was supposed to suffer so others could get better.

I thought my suffering made me excel at my work using my tremendous compassion and patience for others … unlike my intolerance for myself. In the quiet moments, I felt worthless, undesirable, and found a multitude of ways to pick myself apart.

I made sure I hid my inside turmoil.

I wasn't good enough …

I wasn't worthy enough …

I wasn't smart enough …

I wasn't pretty enough …

Even my "good body" was not enough. *I just wasn't anything enough.* I would struggle internally with wanting to be thinner. Since I could not go too long without eating, I resorted to binging and obsessive exercising. I hid behind my athleticism—if only I were thinner, I would be happy, I would be all right, my life would be better, etc., etc., etc. But the "mores" took over: the more anorexic in my thinking … the more I binged at night to get away … the more I needed to exercise to get back my thin body … the more out of control I felt. My answer was to starve myself, believing I was in control of my life. Thinness I admired, but no matter how thin I got, it was never enough. *I was never enough.*

Often, I put music on and danced in my apartment when I binged and needed to relieve my guilt. No matter how tired I was, pushing myself was "my normal" —no matter what time it was. My day was planned around my workouts before work, during work breaks, after work and at night, my sedatives, and my sleeping pills.

From the outside, I appeared to be living a healthy lifestyle. My insides were a different matter. Any compliments received for what I did or how I looked only served to reinforce my lie.

My need to do this was becoming increasingly clear. Slowly, I was drowning. Where once all of it gave me relief, it was now becoming a prison in which I was trapped. Nothing worked to quiet me. I no longer believed I was living. Frequently, I told myself this is not normal and thinking there is a normal and I am not it.

I gripped tighter and tighter to my addictions, my life raft. Thoughts of suicide surfaced—the same thoughts that swirled around me in my twenties. The option of dying felt like an escape from my emotional pain and turmoil. How would my family feel? I pictured my funeral but could not relate to people crying over my loss—why would anyone mourn my death? I did not care if I lived or died. I would picture a car hitting me while bike riding; a car crashing into me while driving; driving over a bridge while imagining driving my car over the side; or while I was on the freeway driving into oncoming traffic. Instead of feeling alarmed when these fantasies surfaced, I felt relief, knowing if any occurred, my pain would end.

During my first year in San Diego, I also had to study for my licensing exam. It had been quite some time since I read and studied. Thoughts of not passing kept circulating in my mind, telling myself that I'm not smart enough to get through it, even though I passed in New York and had been in the field since 1979. I was riddled with self-doubt and nervous about concentrating on studying. I convinced myself that passing the exam in New York was luck, even though I was confident in my work with people. Being confident with others conflicted with my lack of confidence for what I could do for me. It was a maddening struggle.

I was nervous when I signed up for a class to prepare for the exam. I thought everyone was going to be smarter. Once again, I was that little girl in the slowest reading group in second grade. My insecurity followed me to San Diego. Did I really think I could be different out here? I was the same fraud I was in New York, getting them to believe I was smart and knowledgeable. If they only knew I never read ... how smart would they think I was now?

What a fraud I was.

Driving to Sacramento with another therapist who signed up to take it as well, my self-doubts took over. As we approached our destination, I felt like a scared little girl hiding in an adult body. I was barely able to concentrate and nervous. I saw myself as a child with my reading difficulties. My difficulties in school were parading around in my brain. *How the hell was I going to take a written exam as well as oral? Who would believe I knew what I was doing?*

In front of a panel of people, I became my competent self and pulled it off. It was as if I stepped out of my scared little girl and stepped into my professional adult self. Why couldn't I hold onto being smart? My sudden shift in moods or beliefs were perplexing: one moment, I was a competent adult, then something unbeknownst to me would cause me to shift into another part of myself that was dumb. Suddenly, I became dumb with feelings of worthlessness but wasn't I just feeling smart? Once I felt dumb, I must wait to shift back into smart which I believe was far in the distance. *How come I could not hold onto being smart?*

Hitting Bottom

What became scary was my thought that the changes I was experiencing were harder to hide. I felt more and more visible as if a spotlight was shining on me. No matter what I did to dim the light, I could not shield myself adequately. I kept seeing glimpses of myself which led to the questioning of my behavior. I began seeing with clarity my pill-popping, my extreme exercising, my obsessions with men, with how I looked and whatever else there was to notice at that time was not normal.

The "truth" was ever more present. It was in front of me ... I HAD A PROBLEM. Nothing was making sense and I was losing grip on myself, or what I thought was myself. I didn't even know what myself was anymore.

The manager of my apartment complex became a friend and confidant. We started talking, and I revealed my pill usage to her. I was shocked when she told me she was a recovering alcoholic. Listening, she would let me insist that I could stop at any time—I just had to put my mind to it.

My will to live was failing.

I did want to stop and despite all my will power and belief that I could, I ... could ... not. I started talking about how hard it was and how discouraged I felt about not stopping. Slowly, she revealed her story with alcohol and her inability to stop without a twelve-step program. I felt shame being a therapist and in the same situation. What a fraud I was.

I felt as though I was living in two different worlds. My outside world looked as though I was living a good life, successful and well-rounded. My inside world reminded me I was worthless and filled with self-hatred. I was living a lie, but did not have the courage to admit this to anyone until one night when I surrendered. I needed help.

One night, I was about to take my sleeping pill. Instead of putting it in my mouth, I took the whole bottle and dumped the rest of them in the toilet bowl.

For months, I had been trying to cut back, so I was not taking as much as before. I also decreased my sedatives and increased my exercise schedule. I lied to my doctor about my increase in usage, but asked about cutting back. I found it was extremely difficult although I would not admit this at the time. This had been going on for at least six months with my anxiety increasing as well as my lack of sleep. I kept telling myself I am strong, I can do this. I did not think I was addicted. But as time went on, the struggle became harder and harder. I was losing concentration, feeling an increase in desperation and nights were intolerable. Worst of all, I was not able to push myself, no matter how hard I tried. My will to live was failing.

After I dumped my pills in the toilet bowl, I sat down on the floor and sobbed. I cried in a way I never had before. And, I felt angry that I just flushed my pills and had no way out. I thought of other ways to kill myself like slitting my wrists, running in front of a car or ordering another kind of pill. I remembered exactly how I felt ten years earlier taking a bottle of pills and having my stomach pumped and being hospitalized. Here I was again, knowing that I was worse than the first time

I tried. I was also very aware that nothing in my life was better. That I moved 3000 miles from where I grew up, only to be in the exact same spot as before. WANTING TO DIE.

My life flashed before me. Not what I accomplished, but the depth of emotional pain that I lived in. I had reached my emotional bottom, almost paralyzed in my thinking. I knew I could not go on like this. I needed to change my inside pain. If I didn't, I would die. I couldn't continue another day.

After several hours on my bathroom floor, I got up and went to my front door and opened it. I walked across the complex straight to my manager's door and rang her bell. I was being driven to this moment with a determination and will to get help in a way that I never experienced before. I became the marathoner, running to the finish line. This time, I was determined to conquer my deep emotional pain, not run from it.

Answering the door, she smiled and said, "Come in." I sobbed openly and said I wanted to either kill myself or change, still not knowing what I was looking for, but willing to be guided. This was my first experience in my spiritual awakening. I knew I needed help. My self-reliance was not working.

I admitted to myself that I did not have the answers, and that no amount of a substance or running another 3,000 miles from San Diego to somewhere else would fix my insides.

She handed me the phone after she dialed the Narcotics Anonymous hotline. When I heard the words "Narcotics Anonymous," I was barely able to say hello. I got quiet and the anonymous person talked. He said, "I know how hard it must be for you to make this call."

That was all it took. My sobbing increased, and I couldn't stop. He just listened, and I knew it did not matter why I was crying. Just that I was on the phone with this stranger, who was willing to listen. I believed he knew the why then ... even though I did not.

Finally, the crying stopped, and we spoke. I revealed my pill usage; of my desire to stop and how scared I was to live my life without them. I felt and sounded like a scared little girl. I told him how ashamed I was being a therapist who was falling apart. "People who attend twelve-step programs come from all walks of life," the kind voice said. He added, "The only thing that matters is the desire to stop. Not what we use or how much we use, only the willingness to not pick up."

We talked about addiction and my belief that if I was not using heroin, I was not an addict. That came from growing up in a neighborhood where a group of older guys who came from wealthy families were heroin addicts. Obviously, I wasn't that bad.

After all, I was still working, still had money, and from the outside, looked good. At least I thought I did. He said, "It is not how much you use, or what you use, but your desire to stop." I related to this and felt relief. Maybe NA could help.

He asked, "What meeting location would you like to go to?" I could have said anywhere but being the "high caliber professional and world traveler" I felt I was, I said La Jolla, where the rich live. I was not going to a place where drug addicts hang out, and I might be recognized as someone's therapist.

I thought of myself as a high-class addict, not blue collar. After all, I came from Long Island, a very nice neighborhood and a good home life. I had my so-called standards. At the time,

I was serious. Today, I laugh when sharing my story about hitting bottom.

"There is a meeting in Pacific Beach that is close to where you live," the voice said.

Taking down the address, my manager said she would take me to my first meeting the next morning. I heard her words just before I passed out on her couch.

CHAPTER FOUR

My Mother … What I Saw Wasn't What I Got

Bewilderment and doubt
surrounded "me" around her.

My mother lived 40 minutes away, and I began to spend
time with her. At no time did I talk about my increasing terror
and trapped feeling with her. I just lived with it. Instead, I
increased my exercise since nighttime binging escalated, as well
as my obsession with getting "fat." When I was at her house,
I talked about scuba diving and focused on all that was good.

Growing up, I had to "put on" a happy face or else she would
ask questions like, *what's wrong?* This question would set off
anger since I knew she did not want to know what was really
bothering me. I would think *why
do you ask?* And then, immediately got irritated. Then I watched
her curl into herself, wounded by
my tone. Now the "bad guy," I wondered why I would want to
scream at her. My reactions were so consistent, but I could not
put my finger on why.

**Can I believe what she
is telling me right now?**

Driving home, I thought about my interactions with her
and ended up feeling like I did not want to live, hopeless with
thoughts of suicide. As soon as I got home, I would binge
frantically to ward off the discomfort in my body—binging did

the trick. What followed was feelings with guilt over eating, fear of getting fat, food obsession and then my push to exercise it out. I was frantic to stuff myself and frantic to rid of it and easily saw how other people used this with bulimia, binging and throwing up. I was different. It was not the same as me.

I had become a mystery to myself, longing to know who I was. And, who my mother was. I always watched her so carefully— looking for inconsistencies, wondering if she were telling the truth. Even asking myself, *can I believe what she is telling me right now?*

I wanted to accept what she was saying but mistrusted every word. *Why?* To everyone, she appeared so normal—she was engaging, funny, and people of all ages loved to talk to her. I would study her while she was engaged in conversation with someone, wondering, *what did people see that I didn't?* Maybe I had her all wrong. Maybe she was "who" people saw. *What is wrong with me that I did not feel the same way?*

At times, she seemed so warm and loving. I felt so confused about her and felt disoriented in her presence, wanting to make sense of myself in her presence, yet my extreme guardedness blocked me. What was my truth? It seemed so clouded, like my brain was becoming.

Confusion about her became my norm and I felt crazy in her presence.

I was confused and doubted *me* around her. If she was what everyone believed her to be, then I must be wrong. When I thought of being with her, when I was with her, I always compared myself to her … never wanting to be anything like her.

Whenever she saw me, she would smile and throw me a compliment that did not feel real. If she said my hair looked pretty, I would respond, "No, it doesn't—it's dirty," or "I need a haircut." If she complimented my clothes and how they looked on me, I would respond with a negative remark about how I looked. Her compliments always triggered my mistrust. *Can I believe her right now?*

I knew she greeted everyone with one of her compliments as well. When she said someone looked pretty, my head said, *Liar. She doesn't look good.* I would silently pick apart her compliment to dispute what she said. Internally, I wanted to scream. *Doesn't anyone see what I see?*

Confusion about her became my norm, and I felt crazy in her presence. She seemed so warm and loving. My truth became clouded as my brain had become. I wanted to make sense of myself in her presence, yet I remained so guarded that, I could not. Bewilderment and doubt surrounded me around her. If she was what everyone believed her to be, then I must be wrong. Maybe crazy? I always compared myself to her, while not wanting to be anything like her.

She was highly judgmental of people, although few knew it. I would listen to her compliment them, and then when that person was not around, shred them about what they did, said, or wore. I would think, *Didn't she just say how good her friend looked?* She sized people up, always approving or disapproving of their body, style of dress, if their clothes looked expensive or cheap. As she did this, I carefully listened. Wondering the same thing repeatedly ... is she telling the truth now? If she says she likes something or someone and a few minutes later, states her dislike, what can I believe about her?

On the outside, she was warm and fluffy. At times, she was like a magnet, drawing others to her. *Don't be fooled,* I would tell myself. Inside it was a different story. *If only they knew,* I would say to myself.

This was a constant mantra in my head. *If only they knew … knew what?* I would wonder. Because of my dissociation and amnesia, I could never answer this consuming question that I silently repeated in her presence. If only she knew … if only she knew … if only she knew … over and over again, and always … *if only she knew what?*

Every time I greeted her, I felt obliged to give her a kiss, and of course, a big smile. As I did, leaning down to kiss her cheek, I could feel my body turning numb, as if I was a robot. No matter how I felt, I would smile when she asked how I was doing, never knowing how to answer. My usual response was to raise my shoulders up and down with my body language conveying all was fine. Sometimes, with my shoulders raised, I was saying inside *I don't have a clue.* Sometimes I thought *what do you want to hear?*

The reality was that since I never believed her, I never told the truth. I knew … I just knew that the truth would kill her. But what was the truth, when I didn't know what it was myself. I just knew there was something. I was sure about this, unlike everything else.

Always asking myself the same question repeatedly. Censoring my truth, covering my intelligence with the words and thoughts: *I don't know.* Frustrating her by not answering directly. And always watching what I would say and how I would say it. I did it so much that I lost what was important to convey. I would become tongue-tied and unable to continue a sentence, space out or get confused. *Fight-or-Flight* always kicked in. I had to stay put, but inside, I wanted to run away. I was afraid of her seeing inside of me as if I believed she could.

Food thoughts were always with me, along with obsessing what I would eat, and wondering what was in her cabinets. Did she have anything good to eat? I went to her refrigerator to check, then opened cabinets to look inside, thinking about what I would pick at. This was eating disorder behavior—I knew that, I worked with people who had it. Yet, why didn't I acknowledge it?

I would consume myself with food thoughts so I could block out all the discomfort my body experienced. If I binged even a little, I was obsessed with guilt, the fear of getting fat, and feelings of shame. Was it because I was using this to get away from her and myself ... or was there something else?

My belief was that only I was able to attack me.

Whatever my reason, it worked. I felt protected and sufficiently covered up. Now I was in the comforting familiarity of my eating disorder. Even though my stomach felt bloated, my body felt numb, and my mind was consumed with thoughts of ugly, disgusted and self-hatred after my binge. Yet, it comforted me somehow and I could quiet myself down.

Nothing could get me now. I felt sufficiently armored mentally to be around and with her. I believed only I was able to attack me. It created some measure of being in control even though

I simultaneously was out of control. I would tell myself that it was better for me to hate me, than for me to hate her.

In reality, as I pretended I was happy to be with her, it took a lot of energy. Quickly, I felt exhausted within minutes of being in her presence. Automatically, my response was to shut down with her. She carefully watched me as well and sensing her scrutinizing everything about me. My self-consciousness rose in her presence. My body movements became rigid. My thoughts were in check. I was prepared. But, prepared for what?

What was wrong with me? How could I so mistrust someone … someone who had been the perfect mother as I grew up? Is the *something* that is buried inside me, my mother?

CHAPTER FIVE

Was My Life a Lie?

*My life had become
a Nancy Drew mystery.*

MY BELIEF in having an idyllic childhood did not match with my being a drug addict in recovery. Every time I said, "Hi, I'm Lori, and I'm a drug addict," I heard myself and wondered, *What else about me is a lie?*

Deep down, I knew that something was very wrong. My work identity was completely different than my nighttime one.

By day, I functioned well, felt smart and capable. When work ended, I quickly became incompetent and unsure—questioning myself to the point of immobilization and unable to make decisions. I would then reach out to fellow addicts to regain some stability.

At night, I could not imagine getting up, getting dressed and facing the world the next day. It was such a disparity between functional and non-functional. But when the sun came up, I became Superwoman, putting on my costume, and ready to face the day.

I thought, *Will the real Lori present herself?* And then there was the screaming in my head, saying, *who the hell am I?*

I began having a recurring nightmare that I had been haunted by ten years earlier. In my dream,

> I am in a rowboat at night in the middle of the ocean with little visibility. Sharks are circling, and I can see their fins. I know at any moment that I will be attacked. My terror feels ice cold, dark and alone. The sharks feel evil.

I became aware that this same evil lurks in the shadows at night in my apartment. Nighttime has become synonymous with evil and evil things happening.

My bedroom felt like an evil place ... my living room couch became my resting spot, with my back against it as the front of my body faced out. I had to make sure no one could grab me from behind. Of course, lights had to be on and I had to be on the alert—watching, always making sure no one could get me. I must keep my arms close and snug to my body. I could not have an arm extended over the couch. It felt that sharks were circling in my living room and ... *I believed I was crazy.*

There was something very bad in my midst.

An image opened to me after four months of recovery within the Narcotics Anonymous umbrella.

> I saw myself sitting in the corner of the hallway right outside my bedroom door. I was eight years old and frozen in terror with alligators about to enter the hallway.

Why was I sitting there?

Little Lori needed help. I knew it was late at night. I should have been in bed sleeping. Why was I alone and unable to call out, to yell for my parents? Parents who I perceived could be trusted, offer safety, and wanting to protect me. A haunting question surfaced: *Was I lying to myself about my family life?*

Who and what was I terrified of? Every night, this image and thought were revisited. The therapist part of me was watching and trying to interpret what was going on, to make sense of it all. What I did know with unwavering certainty that my use of sleeping pills for ten years was my solution to living in terror. When I saw me as the little girl sitting in the corner, I knew this terror was real. I did not yet know what she was terrified of, just that she was indeed terrified. But of what?

There was something very bad in my midst. Would the truth become a comfort when I found it?

Compulsive masturbation entered my memories. I talked about this with a colleague who was my friend. I described to her that I remembered being in third grade and masturbating under my desk at school. I put a sweater over my lap and proceeded to stimulate myself. Although I did it regularly, I was never caught. Masturbating after school in my room and at night before I went to sleep became part of my routine.

I was looking for clues to make sense of myself.

In my practice, I read that children masturbate compulsively because of being overstimulated by an abuser. It was a way for a child to self-soothe. *Why would I need to self-soothe?* The more I read, the more confused I became. Simultaneously, I developed an obsession to figure this out.

As a teenager, Nancy Drew mysteries were a favorite read, particularly the *Hidden Staircase*. This piqued my interest. When I got the book, I read it and pictured myself terrified in my room at night while reading it. I was looking for clues to make sense of myself. Was my life a Nancy Drew mystery? Was I living in a hidden staircase?

Jigsaw puzzle pieces were now spread out in front of me. How was I supposed to put this together without a picture to guide me? Multiple pieces were surfacing without a clue as to how each went together.

Approximately a month after the image of me sitting in the hallway, another appeared. Now I was in my bedroom at night.

More questions arose. Why am I lying in bed huddled under my blanket? My eyes are wide open; I am frozen in fear. The darkness is alive and growing. Large shadows are lurking, waiting as if they are pausing patiently to seize me in their "grip when I don't suspect it. The colorful butterflies on my wallpaper turn black, alive and big, flying above me and at me. My dolls are staring at me with round black accusing eyes. I know they see something that I don't want to see, as if they have a secret.

The alligators are crawling out from under my bed. I can hear their big teeth smashing against each other, drooling and waiting to eat me. I want to scream for help, throw the covers off and run to my parents' room

but I cannot move. Fear grips me ... my breathing is
sporadic. The darkness engulfs me.

What does this all mean?

Here I was. I'm 37 and felt the same way in my apartment as I
did as the eight-year-old lying in my bed at night. The 37-year-
old Lori had to be entirely covered by a quilt, no extremities
exposed regardless of how hot it was. Creepy, crawly sensations
were felt when any part of my body was exposed. My arm could
not be hanging over the side of the couch. I felt too vulnerable,
as if a monster were living below and would pull me into its
mouth. Shadows were exaggerated in my mind, so I would
turn the lights on, and keep them on. But that wasn't enough—
no amount of light would extinguish what I was experiencing.

In all reality, I became the terrified eight-year-old in my picture,
all alone, amongst terrifying images.

Every time I went home after work, after a meeting, after an
outdoor activity or a date with a friend or boyfriend, I would
feel the horrible transition, from freedom to imprisonment,
as if entering solitary confinement once inside. Immediately,
I would call someone to be able to settle in, reaching out for
the virtual hand and a voice to tell me I would be okay. Drugs
always made this transition possible. Without drugs, I needed
to connect with my sponsor or recovery friends.

My feeling of an unsafe existence was intensifying. I knew
I was getting closer ... but to what? I could not explain
the undeniable aloneness that I felt ... yet. Because of my
recovery support group, I knew I was not alone. But I could
not shake this experience.

As my understanding unfolded, I remembered having a repetitive dream as a child. In it, I am desperately running down the street at night going from house to house. I'm knocking on doors, yelling out for someone to let me in. I had to get away from the mummy or a very large ape, which was chasing me. I knew I would be carried off or eaten, never to be seen again if someone didn't come to my rescue.

Now, the understanding of the previous picture is coming to me. Once again, I am sitting in the hall, terrified.

> I make it out of my room. The alligators don't follow because they only live in my bedroom. I see them peeking out my door watching me, wanting to gobble me up as I crouch in the dark with my arms wrapped tightly around my legs.
>
> My panic won't let me move; I hold my breath. I sit as quiet as a statue. My eyes are closed because I don't want to see the big ape from my dream. *It* lives underneath the stairwell down the hall.
>
> Although I am on the second floor, I must pass the stairs to get to my parents' bedroom where I believe I will be safe. The ape wants to grab me and pull me down into its cage. I want to run back to bed but at the same time I want to run to "Mommy's room."
>
> Can I jump out of my skin—will it make me safe? I can't ... I sit frozen. Paralyzed in fear.
>
> I'm so tired and wish I can be in my bed sleeping. I want to scream but I don't want the ape to wake up. Instead, I scream really loud in my head.
>
> *MOMMY, HELP!*

And then my adult Lori steps in. I needed for my childhood nightmares to disappear … forever! Will analyzing the dreams' meanings bring me clarity? I prayed that it will. I craved an explanation; I craved the truth. Something terrible must be buried in my subconscious. That's what I now believed.

CHAPTER SIX

The Big, Hairy Ape

I sat in the corner of the hall
for what seemed like hours
trapped in terror.
Too afraid to go back and
too afraid to go forward.

THE THERAPIST IN ME was obsessed with the meaning of
the sharks, alligators, mummy, and big ape. At first, writing
became the portal where I worked on my recurring dreams.
I wrote as if I was playing the part of each character—after all,
they were my creation.

My writing felt and read like what it was to terrorize Little
Lori. When I wrote as the ape, I had no regard for her—anything could be done to her since no one could stop me. And
then I wrote as the little girl and her
terror. As I was dialoguing between   **My dream was real.**
the big ape and my Little Lori, the
therapist in me tried to understand the meaning of the terror
that flowed out and through my writing.

It was so overwhelming to have puzzle pieces of memory without
a big picture. When I closed my eyes, I could visualize with
clarity the scenes that would later unfold in my drawings and
paintings. I was very new to spirituality and the twelve-step

higher power. Yet, I asked the universe for the courage to face my truth every night as I lay on my couch in terror.

Over the next month, bits and pieces were shown to me. I got a clearer image of Little Lori sitting in the hall terrified of the ape that lived under the stairs. I realized that the ape lived in my home and this ape was real to me as a child. He was getting bigger. My dream was real. I knew I was getting closer to the truth but still obsessed with the question:

Closer to what? Why did I imagine a large ape living under the stairwell?

> When I come out of my room, there is a long dark hallway that leads to my parents' bedroom. I know that when I look down the hall, there is a big, hairy ape with arms reaching up ... ready to grab me. I huddle in the corner, afraid.

I sit terrified trying to figure out how to pass the ape without being pulled into its grip. I remembered thinking: *If I walk along the opposite wall will it be able to reach me?* Shadows creep along the walls like ghosts. The ape's breathing is loud in the silence; its restlessness magnified in the darkness. This ape is real to Little Lori.

My mind and body are so tired; all I want to do is just sleep. In my head, I am screaming ... *MOMMY, MOM-MY, HELP ME. I AM SCARED!*

But I know ... when I open my eyes, no one is coming. I am alone in the dark late at night when I should be in bed sleeping. So alone.

~

Unbeknownst to me, I am in a flashback. In real time at age 37, I am suddenly that eight-year-old child afraid to put her feet on the floor—my feet—because the alligators will get me. I have to go to the bathroom, yet I am lying on my couch, too afraid to move. I lay paralyzed, listening to my fast breathing. Suddenly, I get up and find myself in the bathroom.

I made it, but I didn't understand how I got from the couch to the bathroom—some part of "myself" had taken over. However, I accomplished it—this I know and my courageous Superman steps into save the day, moving myself from one spot to another. It was a mystery how I moved out of my immobilized scared self into action. I did not yet understand what dissociation was. *How did I get from the couch to the bathroom?* I cannot remember running in the space in between both.

~

I have a clear image of Little Lori sitting on top of my blanket.
Just as I got off my couch in my living room, a change comes.

> Suddenly I am sitting up in bed. I don't remember
> getting out from under the covers, but I did. My hands
> are covering my face so I won't see the butterflies,
> the alligators, the dolls' eyes, or the scary shadows in
> the darkness.
>
> As I sit huddled in terror, I picture Little Lori standing
> on the edge of my bed. I have to jump into the hall-
> way. My feet cannot touch the floor so the alligators
> don't get me. Instead, I am frozen. Quivering in fear,
> while screaming in my head to get up and go but

unable to move. I am picturing the part of me who is the courageous Superman.

The brave Little Lori can run fast, jump high, ride a bike, swim, snow ski, skate, play sports and climb trees. The Superman part of me "can leap tall buildings in a single bound" and has no fear. This part of me loves to move and never gets stuck. I am athletic with excellent coordination and laser-like focus on whatever I put my mind to.

A stern, inner voice vibrates throughout me: MOVE, YOU HAVE TO GET OUT ... NOW! Superman Lori takes over. Suddenly, I am moving toward the end of my bed with the intention of one huge jump into the hall, leaping over the alligators.

~

This ability to switch into different parts of myself saved me in the nick of time. I saw the Superman part of me at 37 ... as the confident adult: the therapist, the marathoner, the scuba diver, the biker, the snow and water skier, and the goal-oriented achiever with laser-focus ability. I was confident and determined.

But there was also the addict who behaved in unacceptable ways. I rarely read. I could not concentrate and I believed wholeheartedly, I was worthless. The nighttime me was frozen in fear, cut off from the world, alone, believing in monsters, fearing evil shadows, and unable to ask for help.

When I was in either part—the Little Lori or the Adult Lori, I knew the other existed but clueless how I got from one to the other. At the time, I believed that I was losing my mind, not yet seeing that my mind was protecting me.

Within a few weeks, my nighttime journey to my parents' bedroom became clearer.

> I am so tired. I just want to close my eyes and go to
> sleep. I am still far from my parents' bedroom where
> I believe I will be safe, but I must pass the ape. I tell
> myself to run but I know I have to be careful. In my
> mind's eye, I see myself walking with my back to the
> wall very, very slowly.

> I keep thinking: *1-2-3, get up* ... but I'm unable to go.
> Then I think about Superman Lori who is strong, fear-
> less and determined ... and suddenly, I am moving.
> Halfway, I freeze. Scared Lori takes over. I am frozen
> in place, staring at the ape's big and black eyes as
> long, hairy arms reach for me. I am glued to my spot
> with a stern voice in my head saying: *Run, just RUN,*

you are almost there. Now I am running to their door, knowing as soon as I touch their door I am safe.

Thinking, *Mommy will make all the bad go away.*

～

When I was out of the flashback, I knew that Mommy never did make the bad go away. Overwhelming grief permeated throughout me with the realization that I was a terrified little girl who was alone in the dark with no comfort or help.

Then, I sat in that corner for what seemed like hours trapped in terror. Too afraid to go back and too afraid to go forward.

I often sobbed in a heartbreaking and gut-wrenching way. The image of my idyllic childhood was completely shattered. I cried daily, alone, to friends and openly at meetings. The flood gates opened and with it, uncontrollable grief came pouring out of me.

Knowing I no longer had pills to contain me, crying overtook me every time I shared in meetings. I came to appreciate that the pills had been my comforter, my blankie, my protector. Giving them up was part of my grief.

CHAPTER SEVEN

The Awakening ... and My Terror of the Night

I still could not admit to sexual abuse, but I did realize that the shark, the ape, and the mummy was my father. My Daddy.

Flashback

I am eight, but I feel like a five-year-old inside me. I am trying to wake Mommy, but it is hard. I don't want Daddy to hear me. "Mommy, Mommy, open your eyes," I hear myself whispering.

My voice is so soft; she doesn't hear me. I try to pull on her covers, hoping she will move. Daddy is moving, and I hold my breath. I'm frozen, standing still, just like I did when the big ape was in my hallway. So still that he won't know I am here. I take a small breath when I see he does not wake up.

Here I am, a mature, 37-year-old woman suddenly transported back in time to my parents' bedroom. I am that little eight-year-old girl, seeing and feeling as if I am living this in the moment. My terror is real. I know clear as day I have a hard time waking her up. Then the flashback ends as suddenly as it appeared. The curtain closes, and I am in my living room.

The present.
What the hell just happened?

~

The Present

The therapist in me repeatedly questioned myself and to friends: Why was I so terrified of waking my father? Why is it so hard to wake my mother? Then my memory of coming home from college at 18 and saying hello to both. At the same time, I am grasping my amphetamine pills in my pocket. It now was making sense.

I needed protection … from both of them! I wondered about their pill usage. On my visits from college, I always stole pills from their medicine cabinet. Each had pill prescriptions, but it was my mother's Valium I was after. Was she a heavy sleeper or was she medicated? I remembered how she suffered from migraines. What I did know was that there were pills to take. And I did.

What was unfolding in front of me was that my life was a house of lies.

Later, another flashback surfaced. While getting up off my couch at 37 to go to the bathroom, suddenly a curtain opens.

> I'm again a child walking down the hall and see my father approaching me. He is nude. I am frozen, unable to move. His penis juts out as he moves toward me. When I look up, I am caught in his eyes. A grin spreads across his face.

The curtain closes. And I am engulfed in shame.

It was the weekend. I went to the grocery store, but I could not shake the shame. I believed everyone was looking at me as though I were in a spotlight, which led to a panic attack. I ran to my car, drove home and called a fellow addict. I could not shop alone. I calmed down and was able to drive to get fast food. I did not go back into the grocery store without a friend in recovery, my lifeline to sanity.

What the hell is happening?

An undeniable truth has emerged. I was terrified of my father. It seems so obvious as I write, but unless you have experienced the process of remembering after a lifetime of amnesia, it most likely doesn't make sense. I felt my life was a mystery with little clues emerging one at a time.

What was unfolding in front of me was that my life was a house of lies. I still could not admit to the sexual abuse reality that was slowly unfolding. I hadn't connected all the dots … yet. But what I did realize was that the shark, the ape, and the mummy each represented my father. My Daddy.

When I was ten, my older sister and I moved to third-floor bedrooms, an addition that my father had built. I remembered in my teenage years that the ape became a man—a man who would *get me,* even though I now lived another floor up. My brother was born and moved into my old second-floor bedroom.

I now see myself at 13 waking up at night, having to go to the bathroom, but being too terrified to get out of bed as if I had to cross alligator and shark-infested waters to get to my door. I stare at the floor until I can no longer hold back the urge to pee. Running to the door, I stand frozen, unable to step out because I believed a man lived in the unfinished part of the attic behind a hatch door above the top of the stairs. My belief became that he would jump down, rape me and stab me.

The ape was back—it had become the shape of a man … *the man*. My terror resembles my eight-year-old journey to my parents' bedroom and my whispered need to wake Mommy.

Now I am describing my experience at 13, and I realize that my whole childhood nighttime was terrifying.

What happened when I finally got to my parents' room? After weeks of wondering, I remembered being next to my mother's side trying to wake her as quietly as possible.

This is part of the memory of going down the hall to get to my parents' bedroom. I don't yet remember what happened when I got in their bed at the end of that nighttime journey past the ape.

But I do remember at 13 summoning up the courage to run from my bedroom door to the top of the stairs as I quickly raced to the bottom step where I would stop, suddenly frozen … and hold my breath, looking down into the dark hallway for the unseen enemy where the childhood ape used to be. It was as if I lived in a jungle war zone, having to run from tree to tree attempting to hide, and knowing I could be spotted at any moment.

Again the 13-year-old, like the child, summons up courage, and suddenly I picture myself running into the bathroom on the second floor, closing the door and quickly locking it. I turned on the lights and afterward fall asleep on the bathroom rug, too afraid to go back, Feeling safe here at last.

Behind the locked door.

Yes, my home was a house of lies.

CHAPTER EIGHT

OMG ...
I Am Fully
Awake

I kept saying,
"It's my father,
it's my father,
it's my father."

MY BOYFRIEND JOHN, also in recovery, was over one night. While having oral sex with him, the flashback curtain opened again.

> I was a child and my mouth felt very small; the penis too big, gagging quietly, the words: *suck it like a lollipop, Lori,* then the curtain closes.

In a robotic way, I stop, excuse myself and head to the bathroom. Closing the door, I lay down on the mat and silently sob until the sobbing sounds escaped my mouth. John came into the bathroom. Sitting down on the floor, he held me. Gulping, gagging, sobbing sounds emerged from the depth of my soul. Out of my mouth, all I could say was, "It's my father … it's my father … it's my father."

It was late at night when I calmed down, and I called my mother, not caring if I woke her. Words poured out; I did not hold back and told her in a younger voice, "Daddy sexually abused me."

I only remember her asking repeatedly: *are you sure?*

I don't remember what else was said, only that I felt a desperate need to tell her the truth. She had to know the truth … or, did she know it already?

Outside of work, I felt disoriented, in a free fall, filled with shame.

Knowing my father was my perpetrator sent me in a tailspin. I lived in a constant state of panic when not at work. The therapist part of me stepped in to function. Outside of work, I felt disoriented, in a free fall, filled with shame. Yes, I carried his shameful behavior as if I "let" this happen.

How could I have not stopped him?

Where was my mother?

How could she not know that her husband, my father, sexually abused me at night in our home right down the hall?

How did I function as a child?

How was I able to get up and go to school after being woken during the night for my father to abuse me sexually?

I was bewildered and simultaneously "I" made sense to myself unlike ever before. The truth was horrifying and comforting at the same time. I was constantly bombarded with conflicting emotions. Yet, I continued to function like I did my whole life: stepping in and out of different parts of myself. My behavior only made sense when I truly embraced the phenomena of dissociation.

One night when I could not sleep, it struck me that I always slept with my back against the wall facing my bedroom door watching and waiting for that someone "to get me"—that someone was, of course, the ape. After a lifetime of this automatic behavior I felt it when the curtain opened.

Flashback

I'm eight, lying awake in my bed, staring into the dark. I see the tall shadow enter before I see him. *Him* is my father. I know he wants his "special time" with me. I try to pretend I am asleep so he will go away. It doesn't work.

Repeating my name multiple times, he whispers it until I open my eyes. The creepy grin spreads across his face with eyes that want to eat me glare down upon me. Time stands still, I am not breathing, he nods his head, I am a robot programmed to make room for him to lie down next to me.

I sob for the little girl who does not have a choice.

The little girl disappears. The robot part of me takes over. It knows the drill.

~

The curtain closes, and I am now 37, lying on my living room couch on my side with my back against it. I sob for the little girl who does not have a choice. I close my eyes and see my father tall, powerful, in control, and I see me, a terrified little girl, thoroughly helpless.

One night, I see an image of my lying between my parents in their bed. I know I have made it past the ape. When I close my eyes, I visualize my mother waking up as I stand by her side. The *little* me is asking her to move over. Instead, she moves toward me, telling me to climb in between her and Daddy. What I see next is a curtain opening to a scene.

My mother did not move over so I could sleep on her side of the bed. I must go in the middle of their bed next to my father. I am eight. I lie awake huddled close to Mommy. I listen to Daddy breathing and try hard not to move. I hold my breath, I'm still and know if I don't move or make a sound like I did in front of the ape, he won't know I am here.

The cigarette smell surrounds me as he breathes. I smell his body odor. I am engulfed in all his smells, and I hate it. I am so afraid. I want to run back to my bedroom but know I must be still. Very still. He moves, I feel terror and I'm screaming in my head for Mommy to wake up. He moves again and puts his arm around me, pulling me closer. I am in his grip. His body hair tickles but I dare not move. He is asleep,

and I am trapped. I know he won't do those "special things" with me next to Mommy, but his arm feels like a lead weight. It is hard to breathe. I am stuck staring into darkness, completely alone in their presence. The curtain closes.

I am in his grip.

~

At 37, I realize I was alone my whole life. Grief for my aloneness consumes me. At 27, I remember standing in the bathroom, shoving valium down my throat. I can feel as it was yesterday, surrounded by aloneness, barely breathing, and wanting an out. Somehow, my stomach is pumped, and I'm lying in my room in a psych ward, still not knowing how I got there, to that place. All I feel is endless grief. Will it ever end?

It is hard to explain how alone I felt at night. I saw my anxiety increase as darkness approached. Indoors meant isolated from the outside world. Without pills, I was unable to relax, settle in to watch TV or amuse myself. For the first time, I felt my restlessness, aware of waiting and not living in the moment. A lifetime of hypervigilance. Listening for my father's movements in the house to avoid being near him, nightly watching the bedroom door, holding my breath to acutely listen for the smallest unexplainable sound.

I now understood why I loved the long summer days and hated the transition to autumn when the light dimisnished—nights came sooner leading to depression in the endless winter nights. I waited for the light to release me from solitary confinement to freedom. I cried continuously on and off for my loss of innocence at such a young age.

Speed was my first drug of choice My answer to tiredness and hypervigilance in my college years. I remembered always being tired; so unbelievably tired and wondering why was I so tired? I always hated being woken in the morning by my mother to go to school. *I just want to sleep* was my lifetime mantra.

"Daddy" didn't care if I needed sleep when he needed sex. His needs were always more important.

It was a lesson I learned early in life and continued throughout my adult years until I understood that I, too, have needs. Yes, I had needs. Lori needs.

CHAPTER NINE

My Secret Is Out

*My shame was a vulnerability
that I hated and wanted to extinguish.*

WHEN I FINALLY ANNOUNCED MYSELF as an Incest Survivor
at an Incest Survivor Anonymous twelve-step meeting, my
father's despicable behavior became real. I was a child, for
God's sake. My reveal shocked me to my core because now
I was telling *our secret* to a group of people—some I barely
knew. Although I only had a glimpse into my abuse, I clearly
remembered Dad putting his finger to his mouth and whispering shush, his sinister smile, and knowing this was "our
secret." I knew I was not supposed to tell … and yet, I did.

My body felt as if I had put my hand in an electric socket;
it was the electrocution of my father as my abuser. I was in
a constant state of numbing disbelief, wavering between
believing and disbelieving. How could he have done this
to me? How could I have not remembered? How could my
mother not know? And always, *the why* … why hadn't I
stopped him?

**Breaking my silence was
essential to my healing.**

Once "our secret" was out, my fear
escalated. I lived in constant terror
of being killed because "the code of silence" had been broken
… as if I were in the Mafia. It was instilled at a very young age:

"Don't tell." Paranoia set in. When a man pulled up next to me at a stoplight, I believed he would raise a gun and shoot me. I had images of crashing my car or driving off a bridge. Either I was going to be killed or kill myself. BUT … I … TOLD!

Breaking my silence was essential to my healing. Other survivors experienced "kill or be killed" when disclosing *the secret*. The crazy paranoia made sense, a normal reaction to incest. I was not "crazy."

Memories flooded in. I soon remembered him threatening me in different ways:

> "Your mother will leave if she knows you are getting 'Daddy's special love.' "

> "Everyone will be jealous and not love you if they find out how 'special' you are."

As I got older, he warned me:

> "You could be thrown in jail for your bad behavior."

> Or … "You will be killed."

He just had to look at me in a certain way and I knew he was threatening me with *don't tell*. Throughout my childhood, behind my mother's back, he would put his finger to his mouth with a silent "shush" and grin. After telling my secret, I blamed myself. It was my fault; I "turned Daddy on." I "must have wanted it." I was a "bad little girl." I pictured my mouth on his penis; him teaching me at such a young age to suck it like a lollipop thoroughly sickened and shamed me. I couldn't eat;

I gagged and constantly felt sick—remembering that his big fucking penis was in my childlike mouth.

The sensation of it was acute at night when I was in a flashback. The curtain opens.

> I'm eight. His hand is on my head pushing me down to his penis. I'm trying to pick my head up, but he holds me in place. I'm gagging; it's too big! I can't get away; I'm trapped. I'm there, but not there. The curtain closes.

Instead of exploding, I imploded and blamed myself.

Back on my couch, I'm 37 and sobbing, then furiously brushing my teeth, using mouthwash—anything to take the memory away. But the sensation does not leave my mouth. Was it my fault somehow? Why do I feel rage at myself for being abused as if I was my abuser? This back-and-forth rage to self-blame lasted for some time. Instead of exploding, I imploded and blamed myself. I was disgusting; I was dirty. I was ashamed and too frightened to rage at my father. Raging at myself through self-abuse became second nature.

The Shame of It All

Admitting to INCEST, I realized how much I hated myself. Deep down, I believed I was not good enough: unlovable, dirty, bad. But shame was intolerable—a vulnerability that I hated and wanted to extinguish. It lived in the deepest part of me, becoming a "soul wound" that I could never rid myself of—deeper than embarrassment. When I felt shame, I was stripped naked, exposed for all to see. I believed if I could open myself up, people would see a crisscross of thick ugly scars and be repulsed.

This led to self-destruction, self-hatred, even wanting to kill myself. I believed I was not worthy of living.

Self Portrait of My Shame

In my late twenties, wanting the pain to stop and feeling completely alone, I took an overdose of Valium. I lay down in bed, believing I would die, and a relief swept through my body. But instead, I was found, my stomach pumped and I was hospitalized in a psych hospital. My tolerance to Valium had prevented me from succeeding.

When I entered Narcotics Anonymous, my hospitalization made sense. I knew I was an addict and needed a drug program; Narcotics Anonymous was there for me. But a psych hospital? Deep down, I knew I was not crazy, but I could not prove it to myself or anyone else at the time. And landing in a psych ward now added to my pile of shame.

I believed I was not good enough: unlovable, dirty, bad.

The revelation of incest painted the big picture. My feeling crazy was a cover for the truth buried inside me … that my father had had sex with me—repeatedly. No wonder shame was at my core. But then I began to appreciate the survivor in me. That I had really endured constant incest in my growing-up years: went to school; had friends; excelled in school and sports; and dated. An awareness of my strength began to appear … it was the beginning in healing my shame.

What I realized was that no amount of bingeing, exercise, pills, or men would ever rid me of this deep-down blackness. No matter what I did—what I excelled at or how good I was at something—I found a way to discredit myself since I was undeserving. Trying to build good on a foundation of shame was a never-ending feeling of failure. I was built on lies generated from my father … and somehow, I needed to preserve the lies at all cost. *DON'T SEE THE TRUTH* was repeatedly drummed into me from an early age. It was not simply *I will be punished* but, more appropriately, *I will die.*

During my beginning phase in Incest Survivors Anonymous, I had an image of myself in my early teens. I was reading *The Pit and the Pendulum*. As I pictured myself reading it, a flashback occurred.

> The curtain opens. I'm twelve, lying in bed imagining a swinging pendulum above me. Slowly, it comes closer and closer to cut me to shreds. Cowering, I'm terrified of the blade, yet unable to stop it. I am breathing fast, sweating, and scared out of my mind.

Cowering, I'm terrified of the blade, yet unable to stop it.

Then the curtain closes. Now at 37, I see me as a preteen, all alone, coping with a changing body, terrified that getting my period means becoming a woman and not wanting breasts because Daddy will make them his. Even thinking that it would be better to cut them off—letting the pendulum cut the preteen me to shreds rather than succumb to him. This swinging blade occurred for quite a while in my teens. It was a terrifying experience. I huddled under the covers because the blade felt so real. It was only thinking about food that got it to stop.

Food was my friend … and my enemy. To rid myself of shame and terror in the early evening when I was supposed to be doing homework, I would think about what I could eat instead. Then, I would run through a list of foods in the refrigerator, get up, run down two flights of stairs, take a few bites of ice cream, run back up two flights of stairs, then sit down and try to concentrate. If I ate too much, I would do jumping jacks, sit-ups, push-ups and dance moves to rid myself of the food. I never threw up. Even doing this, I still could not settle down. Homework often didn't get done. The "evil that lurked in the night" was a constant distraction. I could not concentrate on anything else but that.

Throughout my childhood, my father paraded around nude. When my parents' bedroom door was open, I would walk in their room and unexpectedly see him lying down without clothes. He enjoyed catching my discomfort, my rigid stance and shame. He always winked and smiled with his "this is our secret" grin.

I believed I must be doing something "bad" for Daddy to behave like he did, even though my mother was embarrassed by his nudity. If he walked out of the bedroom, she would yell in an annoyed tone, "Put on a bathrobe in front of the kids." His response to her was "this is my house. I can walk around however I want."

His response to her: "This is my house.

When I had friends over, I was always scared that he would walk out of the bedroom naked. As it was, he paraded around in his underwear that showed the outline of his penis. My friends would giggle, and he would laugh, while I was consumed in shame.

During the first year in Incest Survivors Anonymous, I had a flashback. Sitting on the beach, I was enjoying watching children playing by the water when suddenly the curtain opens.

I'm five, in our dinghy with three of my friends, and my father is rowing us. His fully exposed penis sticks out of the side of his bathing suit. I'm embarrassed and at the same time, I'm trying to get his attention ... thinking he must not know. As soon as he looks at me, he winks and smiles.

I know to keep my mouth shut and pretend not to see. I'm trapped in this boat, fearful my friends will see, and feeling ashamed.

The curtain closes. And suddenly, I'm back on the beach.

The realization of being a child thinking he did not know his penis was exposed then seeing clearly his wink and smile.

It hit me like a ton of bricks. He knew! He always knew what he was doing! I was so innocent; he was so shameful. The grief at my loss of innocence and unwarranted shame was over-whelming.

My father made it a point when going to the bathroom to leave the door open. It frequently happened when I was in their bedroom talking to my mother while sitting on the bed. He would announce that he had to go to the bathroom. I would automatically start to stand up, thinking I should go. My mother would say, "Don't go, it's just your father." As he peed, he would push the door open wider.

Now, she would add in an irritated tone, "Saul, close the door."

I knew I was supposed to act like this was no big deal since it's just my father. Yet hearing her annoyance, I knew it was.

My mother's words were drowned out by the sound of his pee hitting the water. And I would act as if I was not noticing the appalling behavior. The flashbacks continued. The curtain opens.

> I'm in fifth grade now, and I'm laying nude on my parents' bed with stomach pain. My mother is administering an enema—the kind they used to use with the rubber bag and a long tube inserted in the butt hole. I hear my father coming down the hall. Desperately I'm telling her, "Cover me."

> "It's just your father," is her response to me in an irritated tone. Now, both are looking down at me. I want to crawl out of my skin. Trapped in shame and fear, I must act like this is no big deal.

The curtain closes. The recalled scene has played out. I'm back, feeling alone and the futility of it all. Why did they do that?

Avoid Any Special Attention

In my early recovery from sexual abuse, I entered a competition in the Del Mar Fair. All first-year photography students in colleges throughout San Diego participated. Exposed to underwater photography on my Cousteau trip two years prior, I purchased both an underwater camera and an on-land one. I took a week-long underwater photography class in Belize the same year I was taking beginning photography at a community college. I entered an underwater picture taken on my Belize trip.

When I walked into the building where the photographs were displayed, to my surprise, on the wall next to the winner was my photograph. It had earned a Runner-Up Award.

I was in complete disbelief that my picture was hanging with just one other one "for all to see." Instead of feeling proud of my accomplishment, I had a shame attack. I turned and left the building, unable to walk around the exhibit.

When I went home, I could not shake the feeling of being exposed. My picture triggered a flashback. The familiar curtain opens.

> Now I am eight, walking down the hall and my nude father approaches me. He stops right in front of the stairs, blocking me from going down. I am small and look directly at his dangling penis in front of my face. Frozen in fear, I can barely breathe. He is looking down and I look up. All I see is his drooling smile and hungry eyes. Time stands still and I am pinned to my spot, unable to move.

The curtain closes. In the present, I get why I had such a reaction to my "Special" photography award. It was the shame I felt l ooking up at my father's penis. His special attention was shaming; thus, attention equals shame.

As a young child, I was told that I was *special* by my father, but this kind of *special* had to be kept a secret. I could not tell anybody about "Daddy's special love." Now I understood why my mother's praise was intolerable. If she knew about his special love, she would hate me. His sinister smile, along with a finger to his mouth silently shushing me was ever present.

I must ward off questions and act like everything is normal while I am screaming in my head.

His loving words in my bedroom at night were never spoken outside of my room. He always seemed to be in his own world.

If I were in a room with him while watching TV, I could never concentrate because I wondered if he knew I was sitting in the same room. In those instances, I felt invisible. This invisibility was different than my trying to hide. It was as if I did not exist. If I tried to say something, I would often ask, "Are you listening to me?" Only then did he look up. Once his attention was on me, I would get confused and give up what I was trying to tell him.

After a night of Daddy's "special love," I woke up ashamed of myself and blocking out the night before. I never knew why. I just knew I did not want anyone to see me. I hated the dark, but I was too visible in the morning light. Light was revealing; I did not want to be seen.

Another flashback. The curtain opens.

I'm eight. I go down the stairs to the kitchen after "a night" with Daddy. It's now daytime. The black and white of night disappears and color returns. The big ape that lives under the banister in the hallway is gone. The table is back. I think about how my face looks. I feel sad but try to cover it up. I feel myself walking slowly, burdened by shame. I'm trying to hide, but I know when I get to the bottom of the stairs, I am going to see my mother and sister. My mother will call me grumpy, and I will answer in a tone she doesn't like, saying, "I'm fine."

She does not know how tired I am. I am only eight, but Daddy comes into my bedroom late at night, wakes me up and insists I suck his penis. How does an eight-year-old hide that? Whenever she asks "how did you sleep" or "how was your night," I feel consumed with anger ... an anger that I must hide from my parents. Instead, I must lie ... and she believes my lies. I must ward off questions and act like everything is normal while I am screaming in my head.

As my mother tries to get answers from me, she gets frustrated. She thinks I am being "difficult" when I am merely being "secretive." I ALWAYS see his finger on his mouth ... SHUSH. I get angry and put up a wall to hide behind. My mother choosing to believe I am moody and want to be left alone.

No ... that is not what I want. I am desperate for her to see what the hell is going on in our house ... in my room at night. I want her to know THAT EVERYTHING IS NOT FINE!

When my sister and I sit at our kitchen table in the morning after "a night" with Daddy, I squirm inside when the attention is on me. I feel my mother's attention as a spotlight shining in my face, as if I am being interrogated, always wondering, *does she know?*

As I sit at the table with them, I watched her from someplace deep inside me thinking, *does she see I am hiding something?* I hate it when she is cheery in the morning while I sit steeped in shame. I feel isolated and alone. My sense of invisibility is painful. And there is always the silent scream in my head. *Doesn't she see?*

It is particularly difficult at the dinner table when we are all there. My father sits in silence with a heaviness about him which makes my mother nervous. Out of her discomfort, she tries to get us to talk while I try even harder to go unnoticed, always hypervigilant about "our secret." It is particularly difficult when she focuses on my accomplishments, pushing me to share with him. "Dad doesn't want to know," is my response. "Of course, he does ... don't you, Saul," as she turns toward him.

The curtain closes. I am back and feeling sorry for that little girl who had to hide in plain sight.

I could never enjoy sharing an accomplishment since I feared "turning" him on as well as fearing her jealousy. As it was, my father admired my talents and athletic skill. I could not feel good about what I achieved. Praise from him didn't count.

According to Daddy, I was "more special" than Mom, so when she praised me, I downplayed it. I believed she felt his sexualized feelings toward me because her compliments were followed by a statement of how much better I was at something than her. I always felt she was in competition with me and jealous of me. If she said I looked good, I would say, "No, I don't." If she said, "Lori, you were terrific," I would find fault with it. Her compliments led to self-hatred and a belief I was not special in any way. This was a lie that I told myself until I identified myself as an Incest Survivor. And I finally understood what was behind my behavior.

CHAPTER TEN

Dissociation ... the World I Survived In

I felt I was broken into parts within myself.
I knew each part existed but clueless
how I got from one to the other until
I Identified myself as a sexual abuse survivor.
Dissociation was a brilliant way to cope
... to survive.

WHEN I WAS NO LONGER USING PILLS TO COPE, I noticed myself switching from one feeling state to another—a switch where I had no control and a switch that happened quickly and without warning. I was suddenly a detached observer far away from the moment acting as if I were still present.

My flashbacks highlighted my automatic switching from present to past and back. They were so abrupt that I had to pay attention. Then there was switching from one feeling state to another that was much subtler. Once I understood that I left the moment in a flashback because something occurred that scared me or made me uncomfortable, I started to get a handle on it.

I'm in a good mood. I am walking up to my front door when suddenly I am in yet another flashback. The curtain opens.

> I am 12, feeling happy and carefree as I walk up my driveway in Merrick, Long Island. As I am about to go through the front door, I become a robot. All happiness disappears as my mechanical self takes over. My father is in the living room practicing his guitar. He is in my line of sight, and I must pass him as I walk into the hallway. There is no acknowledgment when I look at him. The robot me steps in, hiding deep in myself, not feeling his rejection.

The curtain closes. I'm back in the present. I feel myself switch from happiness to a robotic, numbing exterior. Reaching for the doorknob, I walk in, smile and say hello to my husband. I am hiding in myself, feeling my wall but I cannot break it down. It is an impenetrable wall only I can see. I feel far away. And he doesn't know.

For the first time, I consciously witness this transition. My happy state disappears. I feel the wall come up; I feel myself far away. It's as if I am a passenger in my own body watching, on automatic pilot, no longer driving. I am compelled to be this robotic self. I do not yet know how this happens. I just know I am no longer happy and do not feel in control of the switch to numbness.

My body knows I must be ready for anything. I must be hypervigilant.

Although this switching has happened for as long as I can remember, I am now witness to this behavior and know that it protects me. This one flashback helped me to understand that every time I go from outside to inside my home, I must put on a protective coat of armor just to open my front door. It was what I did as a child. I lived as if I were frozen in time, as though my father was on the other side of my door awaiting me—not my husband.

Experiencing and understanding this switch in myself was an important and essential step for me to move forward. My shift from happiness to numb was automatic. The action of putting my hand on the doorknob was the trigger. A trigger was a trauma reminder. Unbeknownst to me, this action set off a WARNING SIGNAL. Becoming robotic was instantaneous. *I numbed out.* It was not a conscious thought.

My body knows I must be ready for anything. I must be hypervigilant. I couldn't just come in. My response was not a thought-out action/reaction. Instead, I was conditioned from years of training to mindlessly put on protective gear. It was not a choice. No matter how I felt or what mood I was in, once my hand gripped the doorknob, a set of behaviors took over.

I felt I had lived in a war zone my entire life. I was not only a victim, but I was a soldier as well, trained to protect myself. There was no one to protect me as a little girl. I was up against 37 years of conditioning. I had to learn how to adjust to peacetime.

Triggers were buried in my unconscious thinking. A trigger could be a comment someone made. It could be something visual, something I heard, or something I smelled. My emotional departure was sudden and not noticeable to anyone else. Only I knew I left. Dissociation was my protective shield. I separated myself from the moment. I was not crazy. It was a coping mechanism derived from my childhood sexual abuse. Wow, there really was a method to the madness.

Sudden shift in moods or beliefs would appear. One moment I was a competent adult, then something unbeknownst to me would cause me to shift into another part of myself that was dumb. Suddenly, I am dumb with feelings of worthlessness ... but wasn't I just feeling smart?

Why couldn't I hold onto smart? Once I'm dumb, I must wait to shift back into smart that I believe is lost. Was I ever smart? Can it be found?

My dissociation felt sudden, extreme, and inflexible. One minute, I felt smart, and the next, I felt dumb.. The sudden change occurred without a clear understanding of why. This switch happened so quickly, leaving me confused.

My Rooms of Dissociation

My body housed different rooms where different parts of myself resided. I knew each room existed like you would in a house. When you walk into a room, you step into its interior. It embodies a feeling, an aura, and lends itself to its own experience. A living room is different than a bedroom. One room is for sleep, another is for cooking and eating, and another is for entertainment, etc.

In most homes, rooms lend themselves to a mixture of behaviors. You may bring your dinner into your bedroom to eat on the bed or eat in the living room. There is a sense of freedom that different behaviors can happen in one room. My internal house was different. The only way to enter a room was to unlock the door with a special key.

Once you stepped inside, the door automatically shuts behind you, locking you in. Only a special key can be used to open the door to let you out. You know other rooms exist, but each room is only allowed one behavior and once in, you can't easily get out.

Dissociation felt like each part of me was in a locked room. When I am smart, I am fully in my smart room. Everything in this room tells me I am smart, and I can excel. I don't feel inadequate or stupid because I am not in the dumb room. In my smart room, I am always an adult—professional, clear, purposeful, goal oriented and achieving. I go to sleep in my smart room and wake up in my dumb one. I don't know how I got into this room. I just know I am in it with a shut door and everything in this room points to my inferiority. My slow reading ability stops me from any professional or pleasurable reading—even from reading the newspaper.

My failures exist in this room. I am not good at anything, and I cannot recall all that I have achieved. That is in another room behind another closed door. I don't want to be locked in my dumb room. I don't even know how I got into this room, but now I am stuck. It makes no sense.

Everyone can relate to changes in feelings and moods or "spacing" out. It is the degree to which these changes occur and how locked in you feel. Only I knew how unsettling these changes were and how quickly they could occur. I had to hide as best I could when they did. Addictions helped me. They provided a cover, making it easier for me to fake my way through life. I could act smart when I felt dumb, or act brave when I felt scared. I could act happy when I felt sad, or act adequate when I felt inadequate. If I was locked in my dumb room, I could take a pill that would catapult me to my smart room. It made me feel like I was in control.

Triggers

Like the doorknob, the transition from day to night was also a trigger. When I came off sleeping pills and sedatives, I experienced increased anxiety as the sun was fading. I was conditioned to gear up for nighttime terror. I had to be hyper-vigilant in the approaching darkness because it meant *Daddy* was coming home from work.

I had to be prepared for the unexpected as if my life depended on it. It felt as though I entered the war zone. Suddenly, I was alert for sound; breathing shallowly so I could hear better; watching for sudden movement; feeling evil lurking in the shadows; as if an unknown enemy was about to get me.

More and more, I noticed myself being "taken over" for no apparent reason, switching from one feeling state to another. I was being triggered to protect myself—to not feel, to numb out. No wonder I felt everything, including my feeling of craziness. As painful and overwhelming as it was to admit to incest, it opened the door to sanity.

One important aspect of recovery was my developing an aware-ness of my hypervigilance. I had to label it, to understand the "fight/flight" response that I lived in my whole life. I watched myself gear up at night but had no clue why I was acting that way. I knew I was frightened but when I looked around, I could never identify what I feared.

Once I acknowledged that I was a victim of sexual abuse, it all made sense. My behaviors were the symptoms of Post-Traumatic Stress Disorder (PTSD). These behaviors were not in my DNA makeup. They were learned behaviors from my father's continual sexual assaults. They were not who I was but how I coped and what I had to cope with. My reactions were normal for a victim of incest. I had every symptom of PTSD—including my ability to dissociate from myself—but I hadn't realized it.

I had endured so much pain over my loss of innocence ... and had pent-up anger, too. I was never a child. I wanted to scream and rage at both my father and mother for this and doing such extreme harm to me ... and, I discovered later, to my brother and sister.

I screamed both inside myself and out.

I was just a child.

I was never innocent or carefree.

I was burdened by his sexual abuse.

I was burdened with his secret.

I was burdened by my mother's lack of protection.

I had to keep coming home to my house of lies.

Doesn't anyone see how this little girl is suffering?

My grief sometimes felt unbearable. I had to see my suffering and witness my abuse for real healing to occur. I had to embrace this recovery. For years, I tried to run from myself in a myriad of ways, including leaving New York. What I realized was I had to make my body my home; I could no longer run from me. I had to live inside myself in a different way.

I had to understand my dissociation. I slowly began to appreciate how skillful I was at hiding from my father's abuse and the effects it had on me. My ability to lie to myself was perfected. Repeatedly, I asked myself:

*How did I switch from being in the moment
to "going away" from the moment?*

What were my triggers?

How could I lie to myself?

*How did I learn to deny
what was happening as it was happening?*

*How did I learn to leave my body
and go to a safe place far away?*

Before I could answer these questions, I first had to admit that the story I told myself and others about my childhood was not entirely true. I grew up in a house of lies. I only believed the pretty version of my home life.

My Perfect Childhood Was an Illusion

Up until I came out of denial of my father's abuse, I described growing up in a loving family on Long Island, in a *really* nice home in a *really* good neighborhood. I portrayed my upbringing as fun and adventurous. At seven, piling into our station wagon with luggage and skis, heading up to Hunter Mountain where we had a lifetime membership to snow ski. We did this throughout my childhood every weekend in the winter. My father rented a place to stay with my uncle's family who lived close to the ski resort. I became a seasoned skier and fell in love with it.

My House in Merrick

As well as skiing in the winter, my family went hunting on weekends during the season. It was always fun and exciting to drive up the mountain in a Jeep and camp near my uncle's cabin deep in the woods next to a beautiful stream.

The summer months were filled with weekend boating. We owned a speedboat that was docked across the street from our house in a channel that led to the open bay that led to the ocean. I learned to water ski in elementary school. At different times, we camped on the beach and spent weekends water skiing. As I got older, my father bought a large cabin cruiser that we took to the bay to anchor alongside my parents' friends, who had boats. Other times we went deep-sea fishing. When I was older, I loved to sit on the bow of the boat with my legs hanging over, holding onto the railing as waves covered me.

During the summer weekdays, we went to camp where my mother was the head counselor at a large day camp in Oceanside, Long Island. Both my sister and I attended every summer from elementary school until I was old enough to work. My brother attended as well. I took swimming, row boating, canoeing, sailing, archery, and water skiing, which my mother taught prior to assuming the head counselor position. We went on camp canoe trips down the rapids, had camp sleepovers, did art, plays, and a variety of sports.

I eventually taught swimming to young children who were afraid of the water, and my sister became head of sailing as well as taught archery. My sister and I often went on sailing races on the Long Island Sound with friends that owned large sailboats. Other weekends, I went skiing with friends who owned ski boats.

While this was very much my reality growing up, it became my only reality—the story that my family told. My mother was great at portraying our colorful and idyllic upbringing. The black and white of sexual abuse was hidden underneath.

The storybook version helped me block out my father's abuse. Blocking out is something all sexual abuse survivors do in one way or another because it is too overwhelming to remember. But having complete amnesia was mind-blowing. How could I live, day in and day out, and not remember his abuse? I had years of time blocked out as if I did not exist in those years. To me, those years are best described as a dark hole.

When I finally connected to incest, I realized I clearly saw that as a child I was afraid of the hairy ape in the hall, and in my teenage years, the man above the stairs with a knife. But, never did I think the hairy ape or man was my father. I remembered waking up as a teenager thinking something awful happened the night before, but I didn't know what. It never entered my mind that my father was sexually

I effectively blocked out the previous night of abuse so I could get up and function during the day.

abusing me. I really began to appreciate this thing called dissociation, my brilliant coping ability to survive. I effectively blocked out the previous night of abuse so I could get up and function during the day. This blocking and dissociation are common to survivors.

Although I had amnesia, my brain was able to store painful memories in real time presented through flashbacks. When flashbacks occurred, I was living in the moment as though time travel was possible. I was suddenly that young child or teenager experiencing what the amnesia had blocked. Sometimes small parts of one experience were shown over a period of time until I could complete the puzzle. At first, it felt frustrating to get pieces little by little. At some point, I became more patient with this slow unfolding of memories. I learned to trust this process … that my trauma, whatever it was, would stay hidden until I was ready to see it. And it took me seven years to organize myself into a coherent whole and paint the full picture of my childhood.

The flashbacks and memories were terrifying and painful, but I soon welcomed them. They helped me make sense of myself. When I connected that my father was my abuser, I finally identified the monster in my home: the hairy ape. I remembered being a child in my room when my mother would yell, "Daddy's home. Come give your father a kiss hello." From that moment until the next day, I lived in terror. Every move I made, everything I did, was an attempt to avoid him or remove myself from my body.

I remembered as a teen, watching werewolf and vampire movies and thinking how much I could relate to their night/day life. I related to the feeling of a nighttime journey into darkness but waking up to a different reality. After a night of abuse, I woke up in a fog, not wanting to be seen, knowing something occurred but unable to remember. I just knew I did not want to face the day. I felt dirty, ugly, and disgusting. I felt like the werewolf.

Denial While It Was Happening

As I was trying to understand my ability to dissociate, separating my mind from my body, I remembered my wedding at 21. I revealed to my Incest Survivor Group that my father tongue-kissed me during a slow dance. He picked up my chin, put his mouth on mine and jammed his tongue in my mouth, then whispered in my ear what a beautiful young lady I was. I remembered thinking in shocking disbelief, *did he just do this?*

I left my body where I was feeling, went up into my head to figure out if this was real or not real while it was taking place. I kept asking myself, *he couldn't have just done this, could he?* So, I thought I had imagined it. This was one of my early memories of when a dissociation occurred. Trying to figure out what is real and what is unreal, getting lost in my thinking in order to leave the sensations of my body where it was taking place, feeling thoroughly confused and not trusting myself. When it was over, I didn't have a clue what I felt or thought.

I remembered how often I tried to decipher reality from unreality.

Deciphering real from unreal was further highlighted after the wedding when I remembered being in the hotel room at the airport. My new husband was in the shower, and I was secretly calling my psychologist. I was in a panic and talking softly. "I THINK my father tongue-kissed me while dancing with me during the wedding." The year was 1971, years before sexual abuse was exposed and openly talked about. My psychologist discounted what I said, telling me that he was sure it didn't happen. By the time I got off the phone, I put it off to my imagination, silently thinking *I am so sick for believing this.*

I remembered how often I tried to decipher reality from unreality. My father was visiting me in my twenties after a divorce from my mother. I was home with him alone. I was at the kitchen sink doing the dishes. Out of the corner of my eye, I saw him go into the bathroom, open the door wider and pee. I had a direct line of vision into that bathroom. I stood there in shocked disbelief, thinking: *Did he just open the door wider?* My body then froze, and time stood still. Then thinking, *did he just do what I think he did or did I just imagine it?* I went back and forth in my head until I exhausted myself and put an end to it all by thinking: *This must be my imagination. I must be crazy.*

I had years of training to learn to mistrust myself ... to not believe my reality. I would go into utter confusion trying to figure things out between their continual lies, my father's threats, and my mother's unwillingness to see the truth.

It was all too painful. Only the good stories could be told. My family looked so good on the outside: dressed in the latest fashions; doing fun and exciting things that were envied by neighbors; owning a successful business; my mother a successful college graduate; and having the many friends they socialized with. And yet I was being terrorized in the night by my father's sexual abuse. This day world and this night world with such conflicting discrepancies were too extreme for me to make sense of on my own. I simply thought I was crazy.

I remembered how much people "loved" my mother. At camp, everyone shared personal stories about themselves with her. They would seek out her help or advice. Even teenagers in the neighborhood wanted her help. I was often told what a great mom I had ... that I was so lucky.

So, I thought:

What's wrong with me?

Why am I so guarded around her?

Why do I feel so different from everyone else?

When I was a teenager, I silently hated her as I watched her outgoing personality and her ability to socialize with all ages. She seemed so happy on the outside. I just wanted to scream— doesn't anybody see what I see? What I know? How can she be happy? It led to my mistrust of myself since no one was seeing what I saw. I truly felt crazy around her.

At twenty-one, my mother took me shopping for a wedding dress. I was already living with my fiancé, so I did not want to buy a white dress. I ended up wearing a wine-colored dress that was not a dress, but a lace negligee with a jacket that my mother loved. My mother took it to a dressmaker who sewed in a lining. While it was pretty, it was a negligee—not a dress.

My mother's excitement about this overwhelmed me. So, I numbed out and stopped resisting to shut her up. To top it off, she wore white. Only in recovery did I see the complete insanity of my wedding. My father tongue-kissing me; calling my therapist from a hotel room; my mother wearing a white dress, and me dressed in a lined negligee. Seeing this reality was so painful but, for the first time, I had clarity about all the insanity I lived in.

All the weirdness in my life had resulted in mistrusting myself. When looking back, it felt like I had been hit over the head with a hammer, leaving a huge glaring injury on my skull and feeling the pain. As I would look around, people shrugged their shoulders, and no one admitted that someone in the room just hit me over the head and the hammer was nowhere to be found. I know I was just hit, but everyone was acting so innocent … that I must have made it up. I learned to pretend that what was happening was not happening.

Overwhelmed by Sensations

As a young child, make-believe play came easily to me as it does to most young children. I could create my own fantasy world and enter it any time I wanted to. I could make believe and be any character I chose. Children cross over from their worlds of make-believe and learn the difference between real and unre-

I am too young to be sexually stimulated by an adult. I just want to sleep.

Finger-painting of helplessness (surrounded by beautiful color but feels like painful daggers)

Finger Painting of my father's sexual stimulation. Pleasure and pain all too much.

al, fantasy from reality. As an abused child, I did not. Closing my eyes and letting myself go far away into another made-up world became my survival. Part of me drifted away while another part of me stayed.

All sensations overwhelmed me. When my father stimulated my clitoris by his finger or his mouth, I would squeeze my legs so tight to fight the pleasure that was building. He would tell me how good I would feel while I was trying to resist. I felt my body betray me when the sensations took over and I orgasmed. I was too young to be sexually stimulated by an adult. I just wanted to sleep.

I felt ashamed of myself especially when he smiled at me with his knowing smile, victorious. He even compared me to my mother and told me how much "sexier" I was than her. That same smile displayed behind my mother's back. Our secret. *I hated him.*

Other times, he fell asleep with his arm draped over my little body, pinning me to my spot. I feared moving since waking him could arouse more unwanted attention. I would lie in his body odor, smelling his armpits, smoker's breath and semen, his body hair tickling and itching me.

I could never say no, I don't want to do this.

I perfected disappearing by leaving my body. I imagined taking magic carpet rides up and away from the torture of being trapped. Sometimes, I saw myself on the carpet, flying in an endless night sky among the stars. Or I would picture daylight, a bright sun enveloping me in its warmth. On my carpet, I saw beautiful mountains, open seas, snow, and stunning rays of sun. I imagined a place where I never had to sleep. Where I did not have to be afraid of the night. Where nothing ugly existed.

While I was being abused, my young body was being manipulated. My father created sensations I had no control over. My discomfort was irrelevant. Any sensation, good, bad, pleasant or unpleasant, all felt the same when I wanted him to stop and he wouldn't, especially if it was hurting. I was stuck. Trapped. Held down. Unable to move.

I could never say no, I don't want to do this.

I could never push him away.

I could never stop his slithering snake-like
tongue from sliding into my mouth.

I could never push his penis out of my mouth
when I was gagging, with his hand holding my head down.

I could never stop him from putting his penis in my vagina
in my early teens, regardless of how much pain I felt.

I could never push him off me when he lay on me,
even though I feared I would die from suffocation.

So, I escaped by dissociating. I could detach myself from my body. It felt as if I were floating away. My mind would take me on my magic rides while my body was left behind. The brave Lori who was strong like Superman stayed while scared Lori flew away.

In childhood, it was adaptive. However, it continued into adulthood when the danger no longer existed. I perceived monsters where there were none. I automatically disconnected from situations I thought were threatening without taking time to objectively evaluate them. Now it was maladaptive and did not serve me.

Maladaptive Dissociation

Habitual dissociation was below my conscious thought. It was a constant knee-jerk reaction to my surroundings. One moment I was attached to myself, and the next moment, detached. I experienced leaving my body or *numbing out*. Other times, I felt as if I were watching a movie. When dissociation occurred, everything became foggy, distant as though I was looking through a veil. Since this had become a routine, it was hard to identify when it was happening.

In my relationship with my husband, the man I married in recovery, my dissociation seemed the strongest. We came together after work, at night, when monsters were lurking, and I was hypervigilant. I noticed how far away I felt. I truly lived as if "Daddy" were coming to get me in my adult home. I always knew where my husband was in our house—which room, what he was doing, exactly like I did growing up.

As if an erect penis was my officer, I had to salute and obey.

I shared this openly when I became aware of how far away I felt. I felt safe telling him. We were in addiction recovery together where a lot of our behaviors were experienced by others. There were many people in recovery who had been sexually abused. When I shared openly about this, women always came up to talk about their abuse as well.

Every night I was obsessed with the thought: *Is my husband going to want to have sex?* I was no longer the same competent adult that functioned in my work life. At night I was younger, nervous, and hypervigilant. Not once did I think I could say "No, I do not want sex." It never entered my mind. If we were cuddling on the couch and watching TV, I was in my head wondering: *Will he or won't he want sex?* Then I'd mentally prepare how I was going to ward it off. Nothing existed but my thinking; I was detached from my body. It was the same wondering I did every night growing up. I was conditioned to wait in fear and uncertainty for my father to want sex.

I began experiencing flashbacks when John and I were in bed together. In my head, I knew John was not my father; but my body would somehow be triggered to automatically react fearfully. We would be kissing, and I would be enjoying this when suddenly it was my father's slimy snake-like tongue—not my husband's. Throwing up was all I could think about. I fought orgasming like I did with my father, tightening my body everywhere to ward off the good feeling building until I gave in, followed by shame. Or I would numb out, waiting for it to be over ... never once thinking that I could stop, or that I had a choice with my father ... or my husband.

I was taught to satisfy my father's hard penis. As if an erect penis was my officer I had to salute and obey. With my father, it was suck and relieve, no questions asked. There was no such thing as postponing Daddy's gratification. The drill was simple: Do it ... get it over with ... so I could be left alone. I went into a hypnotic-type trance doing my "duty" but feeling nothing with my father ... and now with my husband.

If I was standing at the sink washing dishes and my husband came up behind me to lovingly put his arms around me, what I experienced was feeling pinned, unable to get away ... and wanting to shove my elbow into him. I'd numb out waiting for his hug to be over. At the same time, I was thinking how horrible I was for wanting to push John away. My mind said, *he just wants to hug you,* but my body was screaming STOP. And I wanted to get away. It was always a never-ending battle between my mind and my body. The painful truth: I was incapable of enjoying a pleasurable moment in real time.

I was bombarded with nightmares, waking my husband when I screamed out and sobbed uncontrollably from sheer terror. Nightmares resembled my teenage ones of being held captive in a concentration camp where I was sexually abused.

Then my nightmares were filled with my personal memories of the night. I was pinned down, unable to move, trapped, fearing death, screaming out loud in my sleep, thrashing in my bed trying to get away. This happened night after night. I was completely terrified, unable to get out of bed to go to the bathroom unless my husband helped me get there. The bathroom door felt a million miles away as if I had to navigate through shark-infested waters. The ape, the man with the knife, the mummy, the concentration camps and the sharks lived in my bedroom at night. I was again my little girl self, completely helpless … and relieved when the night was over.

Finally, I was no longer a victim lying in wait … but a survivor in action.

Staying awake at night to avoid terror became a solution until I slowly started to find ways to comfort myself. At first, listening to recovery talks and self-hypnotic meditations helped to ground me. Spirituality was new, and I practiced praying to a higher power. When I closed my eyes, I imagined my community of survivors and addicts. This action lessened my aloneness at night. If I did wake up from a nightmare, I wrote about it, which helped me to remember. Finally, I was no longer a victim lying in wait … but a survivor in action.

I had to slowly learn to come into my body. I had to stop sex when I felt myself leaving. At first, this was too difficult, but as time went on, I did. Initially, I felt too guilty to stop. Then, it became my right to say no. I was not willing to live in my abuse. I was no longer the child who could not say no, but the adult taking care of my little girl self and of me now. I learned to be a loving parent to myself by not forcing myself to continue in things I didn't want to participate in. Choosing to stop was empowering. It was a critical step to be no longer at the hands of my father.

CHAPTER ELEVEN

Confronting My Father

I was terrified of confronting him.
I had not spoken to him
since my onset of memories.

TWO YEARS INTO MY RECOVERY, I decided to fly back to New York to confront him. I was involved in a county sexual abuse program, Adults Molested as Children, AMAC, where I sat in a therapeutic group with a mix of survivors, perpetrators, and their spouses led by mental health workers. We split up into smaller groups with the purpose of sharing our experiences of abuse from different points of view.

I spoke about my intention of confronting my father and asked the group if I should discuss my abuse with my niece (17) and two nephews (19 and 14). I was close with them and felt uncomfortable withholding the truth about being sexually abused. They knew I was in a 12-Step Recovery for Drug Addiction program but not one for sexual abuse. I had already told my sister, brother, and mother about my abuse. I felt it was important to expose the truth to my sister's kids as well. They needed to be aware.

While I was summoning up the courage to confront my father, I happened to call my nephew to say hello. He sounded nervous, and I heard the hesitation in his voice. I asked what was wrong. Almost whispering, he said, "Grandpa comes into the bathroom when I am in the shower. It feels weird."

I thought *OMG, he's after my nephew!* I knew, I just knew by the sound of his voice and his trepidation in telling me that my father was focused on him.

He was a voyeur, always looking.

Memories flashed in front of me. My father liked to come into the bathroom when I was in the shower as well. If I locked the bathroom door, he got angry, using the excuse that I could "get hurt" if I fell. When he discovered the door locked, he demanded that it be unlocked. It was awful. I would have to get out of the shower, wrap myself in a towel and open the door to his angry face. If his bathroom was being used, he would come in while I was in the shower and pee in the toilet. So I tried to shower when he was not around. He was a voyeur, always looking.

Living nearby, my father was able to come and go in my sister's home. Both my sister and brother-in-law worked so my nephew was home alone, an opportune time for my father. Although my nephew was 14, I knew if my father wanted to get in the bathroom while he was in the shower, it would be impossible to keep him out. His tone demanded the door be opened. He shamed me into submission as well.

Alarmed, I asked, "Are there specific times that my father comes over? And, how does he get in the house?"

"He comes over at different times. And he has a key," my nephew responded.

I was angry at my sister for giving him a key since I had shared my abuse to her and had asked her to get the key back. I told my nephew only to take a shower when his parents were home. I said, "Grandpa should respect your privacy, and it was not okay to do what he was doing." I encouraged him to tell his parents, but he did not want to. And he did not want me to either.

I knew I had to handle this carefully, but I was so overwhelmed at this time in my own recovery that I felt helpless to provide a solution. In seeking advice from my AMAC group counselors, they suggested I call Child Protective Services in New York where my sister resided.

Although I was terrified to call, I could not ignore my conversation with my nephew. I heard his nervousness and discomfort. I felt he was asking for help and I believed by calling his local Child Protective Services (CPS), my father would be prevented from having access to my sister's home. I also knew that my sister, while believing me about my father's abuse, was still in denial—not understanding the severity of it.

My father was a perpetrator! He should not have a key to my sister's house or anyone's place but his own. I had explained to her that it was not safe for children of any age to be around him. But I realized that unless she had her own memories, she would be in denial of such an accusation, the same as I had been. How would she explain asking for the return of her house key?

He greeted me with a big smile but was obviously shocked to see me.

The decision was made. I would go back to New York, confront my father, meet with my niece and nephews to reveal his abuse and call Child Protective Services. No one knew my intentions;

they just thought I was coming for a visit. My goal was to break the silence and stop my father from having access to my sister's home. I believed wholeheartedly that this action was necessary.

I was terrified of confronting him. I had not spoken to him since my onset of memories two years prior. And I certainly did not want to be alone with my father, so I showed up at his workplace. He greeted me with a big smile but was obviously shocked to see me. When he went to hug me, I stopped him and asked if we could go to an office to discuss a private matter. I had a tape recorder hidden in my bag which gave me a sense of power. I wanted to document our conversation in hopes that he would admit to something, anything incriminating. If so, I would gladly replay it for CPS.

I told him that I was in a program for incest and had clear memories of him sexually abusing me growing up. He replied, "You are psychotic. I can't believe you would make up such a wild story." He added, "I'm an adult, and I remember. You were a child and can't remember back then."

His denial did not stop me. Brave me proceeded to describe being eight years old and having to perform oral sex and how suffocated I felt when he held my head on his penis; how I wanted to throw up; how I was terrified every night waiting for him to come through the door when I should have been able to sleep; how he woke me up at all hours of the night; how he made sure this was *our secret*; how my secret created a wall between myself and everyone else; how I had to distance myself from my mother and my horrible guilt at my betrayal of her; how this led to my feelings of shame and self-hatred; how I wanted to self-destruct and hurt myself over and over again because of his disgusting and harmful behavior.

At that time in my recovery, I did not have memories of my younger years of abuse starting at five or the older years of his abuse—11 to 16. He continued to deny my memories of what he did to me. What he did to my sister and brother were unknown at the time. I then said, "I don't need you to admit the truth. I trust my truth about your abuse and what you did to me."

Finally, I said, "I will never see you again. Nor will I go to your funeral. Your sick love affair with me is over."

My Little Lori walked tall, merging into the Adult Lori as I left his office for knowing my truth. And for telling my truth. I felt self-respect surround me as the strength of slaying the dragon became a reality.

The next step was also a big one: the reveal to my niece and nephews when they came to my hotel room. I told them why I had really come to New York. I did not sugarcoat it. I said, "Your grandfather sexually abused me while I was growing up."

I purposely included how he came into the bathroom while I was taking showers in my teens and his demands that I unlock the door for him. I explained my terror of him throughout my childhood and that it was not an option to go against him and how I learned early in life to succumb to him in every way he demanded. I described his threats, particularly that I could be thrown in jail with him since no one would understand our "special relationship;" that my mother would leave me; and my underlying fear that I would be "killed" if I told anyone. I discussed Post Traumatic Stress Disorder and my resulting amnesia and the therapy I had had.

Finally, I told them I had confronted their grandfather the previous day and that I never wanted to see him again. We talked for hours. I was advised not to tell them that CPS was coming to their home the next day.

They were stunned with what I said. Watching my youngest nephew's face and body language, I could tell he was relieved.

The next day CPS went to my sister's house to interview everyone. This did not turn out the way I had hoped it would.

I lived in terror for months. Within hours, I was the bad guy. Everyone pulled away from me. My brother-in-law forbade his kids to talk to me. And my mother told CPS that what I said about my father was not true. She believed that my sister's kids would be taken away. My sister also feared the same because CPS focused on her not protecting her children. This was never my intention. I was only concerned with stopping my father from having free access to her home. It didn't turn out that way. My sister became the focus.

I was fighting for my life at that point in my recovery. I felt abandoned and suicidal. How did I become the "bad guy," and not my father? I didn't know at the time that denial comes into play—and is often the case—when people are confronting incest within their family.

It was not until I got back to San Diego that a renewed fear of telling my secret surfaced. My fear of being killed was triggered for breaking the silence about our incestual relationship, only much worse than the first time. I had horrible nightmares of my father and brother-in-law coming to kill me since they were in a close relationship. They were furious with what I had done. When I stopped at a red light, I imagined a gun pointed at me from the driver next to me. In my reality, I believed I was being followed at times and would drive way out of my way before I went home. I lived in terror for months.

Although I had difficulty leaving my house, I was terrified to be home alone. So, I made a point to be on the phone with a recovery friend for a good portion of each day or attending a 12-step meeting. I knew I broke the silence and was experiencing the repercussions of his threats never to tell. Other survivors of incest described living in the same terror and being abandoned by their families as well. I was not alone in this. It was immensely helpful and comforting to have a community to share my struggles with since I had lost my family connection.

Prior to confronting my father, I was in communication with the Law Offices of Andrew Vachss in New York City, a firm that worked as an advocate for abused children, including sexual abuse and incest. I read several of Andrew Vachss' inspiring articles, which expressed his outrage at the way childhood sexual abuse was handled. I decided I wanted to sue my father in court. Although childhood sexual abuse was written into law by 1976, ten years later it was still a taboo topic, particularly in communities of financial means. I grew up in such a community.

At that time, I had seven years after the onset of memories to initiate a case against him. I was determined to bring my father to court, if for no other reason than to pay for the cost of my PTSD rehabilitation. The years of intensive therapy had been costly. In communicating with Andrew Vachss' office,

I was told that it could be a harmful process to me in court since I would be portrayed in a poor light by the defense. My recovery from drug addiction—and my promiscuous behavior —would be exploited. In short, I would be on trial as well. And in addition, taking perpetrators to court was new.

After I had faced off with my father, the terror I went through, and the bombardment of flashbacks discouraged me from pursuing any legal action at that time. I was too busy putting my life back together. But I trusted if it were necessary for my recovery to bring him to court, I would. During the next three years, I experienced multiple miscarriages, but I was also finally learning to love myself. As a result, I was willing to do whatever I needed to do to get better.

I felt consumed with sadness at the realization of how unprotected I was during my childhood. I had been talking to my mother about his abuse before I confronted him and was devastated by her lack of support for me. Although she told me she believed me, I felt betrayed and now mistrustful of her. I wanted her to at least acknowledge what I had told her. I wanted her to admit that it had happened to me! Even though I understood denial in families of incest, when I was up against my own family, I felt like an outcast.

My sister and I were not communicating. CPS focused on her not protecting her children, and she was made to feel as though she was the criminal, not my father. I recognized her inability to understand the extent of how dangerous my father was because she, too, was in denial of his behavior the same as I had been just a few years earlier. I wasn't the only one that he targeted in our house. Even though I had been telling her my concerns as well as asking her to prevent my father's access to her home, my phone conversation with my nephew brought it to a new level.

I was compelled to act and could not live with myself if I had not. It was a risk worth taking, and I hoped it would help break through the denial. I knew that everyone was suffering from my father's abuse, not just me. Instead, we all pulled apart.

For many years, I fell out of communication with my sister and her kids. They later told me that they had felt abandoned by me. And I realized that my sister had felt betrayed by me because I had not told her that I was calling CPS, something I regret. And I should have shared with her what her son had revealed to me that had catapulted me into action. She also had no way of knowing that after my confrontation with our dad, I was immersed in terror and vivid memories of his sexual abuse.

My feelings of betrayal were beyond description. The sickness of my father's secrecy bound by fear and threats surrounded and imprisoned us all. And the real criminal went unpunished.

My mother and I did not speak for sixteen years. I needed to stay away from her to recover, surrounding myself only with people I could trust. I was fortunate to find two friends in Narcotics Anonymous who were in sexual abuse recovery as well. They became my family, my lifeline, my support, and my strength to recover. Honesty was the code amongst the three of us. For me, I revealed every sick memory and sick secret to them. We hung out together; we spoke nightly. We were involved in each other's lives. Although Judith has passed away, Madelyn and I have remained close. When we are together or talk by phone, we can't help but speak of the incredible strength and courage we must have had to face what we did.

Unraveling abuse was a terrifying journey. I am so grateful to my closest West Coast friends, Madelyn and Judith. Without both women by my side, I cannot imagine having pulled through at that time. I was also able to share what had happened to me with my closest New York friend Jamie, who was extremely sensitive to reading people. She felt my father was "creepy" immediately after meeting him when we lived in the same apartment building in 1982. We were in the pool clubhouse and she remembered his look and feeling his "evilness." I love that she witnessed him and understood my abuse when I shared what had happened.

Recently my sister summed up the experience by saying, "It was tragic and sad that we couldn't pull together and support each other." I agree.

CHAPTER TWELVE

Life After Confronting My Father

The thought that I was safe
was impossible during this time.

THE YEAR WAS 1989, a year of new beginnings … and dealing with more of the past. It was the year that I confronted my father, and the year that family stopped talking to me. It was the year that John and I married. A backyard wedding with recovery friends was planned. No family was invited. The week before we were married, I found out I was pregnant. I was ecstatic since I was 39 and for the first time, believed I was emotionally strong enough to have a child—to be a mother.

The night before our wedding, I miscarried. I was devasted and heartbroken. Our friends in recovery came a day later, and John and I married, leaving for our Puerto Vallarta honeymoon the next day. I felt I lost so much in my life that I owed it to myself to go. I was convinced that the strain of recovering from abuse and the confrontation with my father played a role in my miscarriage. Emotionally, I believed that my father ruined me, which brought about another wave of grief.

So many losses.

We wanted children. I wanted a child so badly. Following the miscarriage, I went to an infertility specialist because of my age and to determine if there was anything that would prevent me from getting pregnant. Both John and I were tested, and nothing showed up. I told the doctor my concerns of feeling that I was somehow damaged from the abuse I had endured. He assured me, saying, "Miscarriages happen. You should be able to become pregnant again."

For years, I struggled with my spirituality and needed something to ground me. Rabbi Harold Kushner's book, *When Bad Things Happen to Good People,* helped. I stopped blaming myself and began to feel that I was not alone in suffering and tragedy. It opened my thinking about women who had babies in concentration camps, in abusive homes, during famine, and other unimaginable circumstances. I grieved as I recovered from my miscarriage by reading and listening to meditations that focused on being grateful and having the courage to face fear. In turn, my spiritual connection was strengthened.

For those living in the San Diego area, the news was filled with reporting of a serial killer in our area in 1990. It came too close when one of my 18-year-old clients and her mother were murdered. Five other girls had already died from the cruelty of this monster.

The night after the funeral, I received a message on my answering machine—a man laughing sadistically. Bar noise filtered in the background. Immediately, the police were called. I knew that both the mother and daughter had my card in their wallets and my warning signs permeated through my body. I was told, "It could be the killer. Both wallets were stolen. Be on alert and take precautions."

The sadistic laugh triggered a deep-down terror in me that I could not calm. I had already installed an alarm system and had decorative bars put on my windows as well. Nothing eased my fear. It was impossible to keep it at bay, and no amount of alarms or bars would help.

The thought that I was safe anywhere was impossible during this time.

The murder triggered horrible flashbacks of abuse where I felt trapped beneath my father and unable to breathe. I believed I could suffocate and remembered his trying to push his penis inside my vagina. The pain was excruciating, coupled with his frustration and anger at my squirming and resisting, and then him telling me in no uncertain terms, "You will do this when you are older."

The Black Hole Appears
Older meant when I turned twelve … and the black hole opened. I wished I did not have to relive this time but knew my miscarriage and the murders opened it up, and I could not deny what I wanted to reveal to myself. I knew that my freedom meant walking through this blackness—the years of 12 and 13 had been a black hole to me.

The thought that I was safe was impossible during this time. I felt completely alone trapped in an ice-cold terror. No one lived in my abuse but me. This created an aloneness that was different than feeling alone. It was the aloneness of being a child experiencing horror at the hands of my father, my abuser— with no one to protect me. Although I kept picturing a man entering my house to rape me, I knew the image was not attached to this current serial killer. It was the image of my father who lived inside me. I could not keep him out of me or off of me.

When I was a teen, I had recurring dreams of being sexually experimented on in concentration camps. My nightmares were of penetration, pain, and terror. I now understood my dreams in my teenage years were really my father experimenting on me by forcing me to endure painful penetration.

My home became a prison.

The darkness at night played tricks on my mind. Suddenly shadows looked like people. If the shadows were close to my backyard sliding glass door, I imagined someone breaking in since that was how the serial killer entered people's homes. No longer did I look out my windows, and I only went out at night if it involved work. My home became a prison.

Enough. I was not going to let fear immobilize me. Enrolling in a police course on self-protection, I was determined to fight back and slay the dragon. Mace spray was always with me. But my nightmares continued, leaving me exhausted and barely able to work. It was clear that I needed more time to recuperate from staying awake, avoiding my fear of shark-infested water and my father's abuse. Daily, I reminded myself that I already had lived through the worst of it, but the flashbacks meant reliving the experience—and that was truly terrifying. No matter what I did, I could not relax.

My closest friend and my sponsor, Madelyn, told me that her brother was a guard dog trainer and encouraged me to get one from the Alderhorst training facility where police protection dogs were trained. I learned that there were family protection dogs that failed some of the tests—tests that were inconsequential for my needs.

FoPo, a two-year-old German Shepherd, became my personal protector. I was instructed to take him home for a month and bond with him, then return to the training facility for "sleeve" drills. It was emphasized that these dogs needed to feel a bond with their owner to be motivated to attack.

We bonded quickly. The outside world saw me as a mature adult. Within, I was a terrified little girl, desperately needing protection. FoPo provided it. I only felt safe when I laid down curled up next to him. I knew he could sense my vulnerability. In less than a month, we returned to the training facility. They were amazed at how well he wanted to protect me. What a relief. For the first time in my life, I believed no one could "get me" or "sneak up" on me without facing his attack. It was the most empowering action I took on my behalf, now knowing that I would go to any lengths to keep myself safe after a lifetime of feeling unsafe. FoPo was there to protect me.

I learned important lessons in the actions I took to protect myself. FoPo was instrumental in helping me to move through my hardest phases of abuse recovery. Previously, I stunted the completion of grief in many ways. When something got too painful, painkillers were the go-to fix, leaving me in an endless loop of numbing. Not using anything to take away my pain allowed me to heal the loss. At the same time, I gained healthy ways to take care of myself as well as protect myself.

I was in therapy at the time and worked on rescue visualizations of my little girl, always bringing FoPo with me to save the day. I imagined scenes where my father was in my bed when the adult Lori forced my father to get out of Little Lori's bed, with FoPo's help. I would picture FoPo and myself crashing through the door, my dog viciously growling and straining at the leash to get to my father. He would look on with terror in his eyes as I took Little Lori away from him. I told him with a knowing strength that he was an unfit father who would never see Little Lori again. Sometimes I would take my little girl away and leave my dog to attack my father. No matter how vicious my visualizations were, they helped me to not hurt myself.

When doing inner child work, I created a safeness I had never had. A safe room was constructed through a visualization for Little Lori. A room was created that had bright warm colors, impenetrable walls that no one could get through and always FoPo right next to her, ready to attack. Little Lori was never alone. I visualized me at different ages knowing I would not allow me to be hurt ever again. FoPo made sure. These images were the start of learning to nurture me and keep myself safe.

For the first time in my life, I felt protected, knowing he would "kill" to keep me safe. It was exactly what I needed in my abuse recovery. Unlike ever before, I was able to sleep with my back facing my bedroom door because I knew my loving protector slept right outside my bedroom. Since no one could sneak up on me, I was able to go into my jacuzzi alone at night. For the first time, I experienced a lessening of hypervigilance, which helped me to relax in ways I never had. I was able to go out at night in my car with FoPo if I wanted to pick something up at the store.

Only an attack guard dog eased this.

Without FoPo at my side, the darkness looked evil, like my shadows did in earlier recovery. No longer did I have to check and recheck to make sure the doors and windows were locked. Even though I lived with John, I still believed someone could sneak up on us if we were sleeping. Only an attack guard dog eased this.

As I continued the process of repairing myself, this led to further actions of healthy self-care and empowerment. I started attending 12-step food meetings separate from Narcotics Anonymous. Although I was focusing on food issues, I felt I needed to do more. I used sugar off and on to numb myself.

I relapsed in food recovery many times. Eventually, I developed consistency and found I felt my best when sugar, wheat, flour, and milk products were eliminated from my diet. Natural grains, proteins, fruits, and vegetables worked well for me. Eating healthy is an act of self-love and self-care that has become very important to me. It has led to exercising moderately, not addictively. Learning how to take care of myself in these ways has been an important aspect in my recovery from sexual abuse. After a lifetime of self-destructiveness, I had to learn kind and loving actions to take on my behalf; something that hadn't happened naturally.

CHAPTER THIRTEEN

The Healing Journey Interrupted

I stopped saying
"I don't know how to do _____" or
"I'm not good at _____."

DURING THE YEARS from 1989 to 1992, I had three miscarriages—each bringing further abuse memories. The excitement I felt at becoming pregnant only to feel the baby's life slipping away connected me to a profound sense of helplessness. Nothing I did could stop this from happening; it further increased my sense of helplessness. My memories continued to surface, whether I wanted them to or not.

After my second miscarriage, I had a desire to play the piano. After playing the clarinet and accordion as a child, I wondered why I hadn't added piano to the mix. My father's sister played, and I remembered sitting at her piano and fooling around ... loving it. Now, memories of the piano as a child danced through my head.

My abuse recovery opened parts of myself that I had blocked in dissociation. It was as if the good got covered up by the bad.

I called my father's sister, who lived in Florida. She shared that my Russian relatives had an array of musical talents. She told me that I had expressed interest in wanting to learn how to play, and she had taught me whenever I visited as a child. I was surprised to learn that I also displayed a talent for art, something that was a mystery to me since I did not remember being musical or artistic at that time in recovery. Then she told me that my ancestors fled Russia with the eruption of the pogroms, violent riots that were aimed at the persecution and massacre of Jews.

I told her about my father's abuse, but I did not learn anything new. I felt that she either didn't know anything … or was in denial. So, I didn't explore my situation any further with her.

After our phone visit, I remembered being in special singing class in elementary school. One of my friends had taken me to a home where all of us were in different phases of recovery. Besides recovery, the common bond was people coming together for spiritual singing. I loved it. Opening myself up to singing led to my pursuing Djembe drumming and Brazilian dance. I knew I had loved to dance as a child and began to have memories of dancing in my basement with women from multiple nationalities and cultures who were live-in nannies in my neighborhood.

For the first time in my adult life, I was bursting with passion.

When my brother was born, I was ten. We had several live-in nannies, but I remember Gloria vividly when I was twelve. She'd invite her friends over when my parents went out. I had so much fun at these gatherings. We all "let loose" and I was turned onto different types of music, particularly drumming, that I loved.

In abuse recovery, I was willing to explore whatever opened to me. For the first time in my adult life, I was bursting with passion. I wanted to sing, dance, and play music in between grieving, miscarrying and abuse memories. And I was overwhelmed because all of these passions burst forth at the same time. I could not sit still and was desperate to connect with what I had lost in my childhood. I needed to know who I was—not who I believed I was to this point in my life. I stopped saying "I don't know how to do _____," or "I'm not good at _____." Everything was a wait and see.

My parents listened to drum music and a variety of dance music from different cultures. And I remembered dancing in the basement with my father and mother who both enjoyed dance. Lindy music became a favorite; I won a Lindy contest at school. Unfortunately, while these pleasurable memories were surfacing, other bad memories did as well, which happened throughout my abuse journey in healing.

The beginning of each school year meant that there would be new clothes. My mother always felt she spent too much, and my father would be mad. In order to ward off his anger at us, she would set up a dress show, and my sister and I would each model our selections. My father would sit in the living room while he watched me walk down the hall, one flight above him, descend the stairs, and move into the living room where he was waiting.

My dance was theirs, never mine.

My mother put music on and wanted me to dance for my father, my perpetrator, in my new clothes. She insisted I do it so he would not be mad and return our clothes. I protested but my mother said, her tone snappish, "It's your father." They both laughed while I danced, saying, "Lori dances so sexy." I was already good at being in the moment while I left my body through dissociation. From their perspective, it probably looked like I was having a good time. What I remembered was wanting to disappear from my father's view … while he undressed me with his eyes. My dance was theirs, never mine.

Music Comes into My Life

In 1990, I started piano lessons. I loved playing, but I felt I needed a teacher who would help me learn to create my own music, not simply read music. At the time I loved listening to Windham Hill musicians and discovered a teacher who played this genre of music. Reaching out, I called. Feeling it was important for him to understand what I was going through and my journey, I shared about my recent discovery of wanting to learn the piano. We talked for quite some time about drug and sexual abuse recovery, years of running away from myself, my miscarrying and my hunger for a deeper connection to *me*.

I shared I had been playing for six months prior to this call and started to sound out a song I titled "Glimmering Light." He asked insightful questions and appreciated my wanting to learn to improvise and write my own music. More than anything, I wanted to feel safe to explore.

He was willing to work in an unconventional way, which was exactly what I needed at the time. I was nurturing my *little girl*. My new teacher proposed ways that we could work together over the speakerphone as well as in person.

When we met at his studio for the first time, he wanted me to sing while he played his sitar, incorporating the music he learned from his music teacher in India. I was shy, but he helped me to relax and told me that he was impressed with my hearing and singing on pitch. I cried deeply. He understood my need to release emotion and sat with me while I cried.

This was the teacher I needed. He was wise and understood my personal journey in healing. After I purchased a handmade sitar that he brought back from India, he taught me how to play and sing with this profoundly soothing instrument. I could lose myself in its simplicity and connect with my longing to be free.

Silence

Memories of my father playing the guitar surfaced. I remembered him playing for hours and listening to classical guitar. While the music was beautiful, I picked up quickly his ability to get so immersed in what he was doing, he ignored everything around him. I often wondered if he knew I was in his space. Memories surfaced of coming home in my teens and opening the front door to him playing his guitar in direct line of view of me and being ignored—not so much as a hello. Yet he lavished his attention on me during his sexual bouts where I was the target.

I did not know how to let down my protective guard.

I wanted to make myself invisible, but at the same time when my invisibility was the result of his lack of attention, somehow it hurt and was terribly confusing. His silence filled the room while I felt alone and unreal. If I needed to get his attention for something, he ignored my questions unless I raised my voice, always a shout, "DAD,

ARE YOU LISTENING?" His eerie silence led to anxiety, a terrible foreboding.

Finally, it made sense how uncomfortable I was around my husband's silence. I tried to provoke him when he was too quiet. I hated silence but only now did I recognize why.

Being so preoccupied with my father's silence as a child, I could not relax into my own activities. I wondered what he was thinking; wondered if he noticed me; wondered what he was doing; wondered what would happen next. I was unable to focus on me. My hypervigilant side went on alert in his quietness to do anything else. I had to be alert to when he stopped what he was doing since I needed to know where he was in the house in order to predict his next move. My life revolved around him in every possible way that it could. I was drowning and didn't know it.

My guard was always up. My perpetual feeling of being unsafe blocked me often from living in the moment—a horrible consequence of incest. When I let it down, it reminded me of war vets who must learn to lay down their weapons, leave the war zone and learn to live in peace. It was what I needed to do, but I couldn't … at least now. I did not know how to let down my protective guard. It was heavy to lug around—the weight of a thick metal shield. I was noticing more and more my trouble breathing and difficulty relaxing in the moment.

The following year I pursued Djembe drumming with a master drum teacher as well as continuing with my piano lessons. I loved drumming and had an ear for drumming rhythms. My teacher visited schools to talk about African drumming. My passion was exhilarating and frightening at the same time.

It was a portal to unleash my rage at my father and mother. Connecting deeply to the sounds of drum rhythms, I literally drummed myself into an injury. I pushed in ways I should not have. My body oozed with a rage that I needed to express. Drums became my vehicle.

Next in my healing journey, I began physical therapy. Although I had always been athletic, I worked with a personal trainer, desiring to strengthen areas of my body that were weak to prevent further injury. I learned how to use weights properly as well as develop a healthy routine.

My grief felt endless and my rage was overwhelming, vacillating between the need to release and hold back.

Having to back off from playing music led me to my awareness of how I pushed myself with no regard to my body's limitations. I was never able to sit still. "Doing" was my way of avoidance. When I did get quiet with myself, I noticed how much I held my breath, my hypervigilance. My body did not know how to adjust to "peacetime;" it was still in the war zone. I was aching in every joint—my neck, my shoulders, my arms and legs—that led to my being tested for an autoimmune disease. It came back negative. I could not deny that I felt myself holding on for dear life in every part of my body as I rode this terrifying roller-coaster of abuse memories, loss, and emerging passion.

Recognizing my need to hold my breath led to my pursuit of biofeedback to develop a better awareness of my breathing. I had been working with meditation CDs at the time to learn how to relax—my guard was still up. It was astounding to see how much I resisted breathing as I watched this feedback on a monitor. I learned this at such an early age, to hold my breath, to be alert, to better listen for my father's approach. My grief deepened, once again connecting to my loss of innocence and the freedom I never had as a child. I was always burdened by abuse and deadening passion.

My grief felt endless and my rage was overwhelming, vacillating between the need to release and hold back. It was an exhausting process, leaving me drained. But I knew I had to continue to walk down this road to get to the other side. I was clearer now about what I lost in dissociation, which motivated me to keep going even though there were many times when I just wanted to give up.

I talked with my personal trainer about abuse recovery, which I did with anyone who I worked closely with. She recommended that I work with a masseur who did very deep massage. I was holding on tight in all my muscles, a long-established way to ward off abuse. Since I was able now to connect to my tightness, I could learn to let go. Without this awareness, it was impossible to identify what was going on in my body, much less address it.

Once again, I had to trust those I worked with and sought help from. I opened up about my personal journey in abuse recovery so he would understand my need to release. As he worked intensely on different parts of my body, I was able to release pent-up emotion. Sometimes I sobbed while he worked on me. I had to let go. So much grief, so much terror, so much rage, so much helplessness throughout my childhood that I was holding in every part of my being. While the emotional pain was excruciating, the freedom to breathe was exhilarating.

In 1991, I had my third miscarriage. I was already devastated from the first two, but after the third, I knew I would not try again. Eventually, we would adopt. I grieved the loss of being able to carry a child to term in my body. Once again, I felt grief over the innocence of my childhood being ripped away as I grieved the loss of a successful pregnancy that so many took for granted. Everywhere I looked, pregnancy blasted me in the face. I saw pregnant women or new moms pushing baby carriages. Any clothing store I was in, maternity clothes would be displayed. And of course, moms holding babies. *Why them and not me?* I tried to stay out of that thinking, but it was hard. The grief was draining.

My trek continued: recovery meetings; therapy; writing daily; grounding myself in my spirituality; practicing being grateful; reaching out to my closest friends who I valued more than anything else; seeking out help wherever needed. And, of course, I continue in my recovery journey.

The Empty Cradle, an organization for parents who miscarry or have had a stillborn child, came into my life. Both John and I attended their meetings and were relieved that they did not say all the unintended hurtful things that people say when you miscarry. In a ceremony, we were able to light candles with other parents as we went around the room stating the name of the lost babies that we grieved. I felt I could experience some closure. I walked around feeling deeply that I lost a child, yet there was no child to show for it. In this way, the grief is difficult to heal. Eventually, I assisted at support groups to give back.

Again, from 1989 to 1992, I pursued different forms of treatment for abuse recovery while continuing my 12-step support groups. I was in therapy at the time and learned in my Incest group about a psychologist using Doriden, a truth drug, to help access memories. I pursued this option after reading about it, talking about it in recovery, and talking to the therapist who specialized in sexual abuse and understood its complexity. I set a date to do this.

I asked a doctor who I knew personally in recovery to assist as well as my therapist while the drug was administered so I would feel safe. My two closest friends, Madelyn and Judith, were planning to sleep over to help afterward. Abuse recovery took time, effort, money, and willingness to do whatever I felt I needed to do to get better. I was determined to free myself from the prison of abuse.

I thought, *did he kill her?*

I came out from that session not remembering much once the drug wore off. I taped it and knew I talked about being 12 and 13, two dark years in my childhood. Gloria was our live-in nanny who disappeared suddenly from our lives. I had vague memories of being on a boat with her, but that's what they were, vague. The tape erased the vagueness, but I couldn't listen to it. I wasn't ready. For months, I had been remembering her, a woman who was hired as my little brother's nanny. At the time, he was three, I was 13, and my sister was 17.

I distinctly remembered my father joking around with Gloria in the kitchen. He would come up behind her, cupping his hands on her breasts and her giggling. Gloria had large breasts, and my father flirted with her when my mother was not around. She flirted back. Before the Doriden session, I recalled being hidden behind a wall, standing on the stairway leading up to my bedroom, listening to my father talk to the police at the door. They were looking for Gloria.

According to the police, she was reported missing by one of her friends. My father told them, "I haven't seen or heard from her. She did not come back to our house after being off for a few days." He added, "It's strange that she didn't return … all her things are still here."

He was smooth, friendly, and cooperative with the policeman. At that time, I did not know why he was lying, I just knew that he was. I remembered thinking *he's lying* while listening to him talk. Then, pieces of scenes flashed before me too quickly to capture. I knew something awful happened that I witnessed, but the memory was not within reach. I thought, *did he kill her?*

This frightened me and provoked a wave of terror the same as when my client was killed a year earlier. I was so grateful for FoPo because I was paralyzed with terror. I was restless, unable to sleep once again and knew something very big wanted to emerge. I kept asking myself, *was my father capable of murder?* The answer was, *yes, yes, he was.*

Wondering, I called the police in Freeport, Long Island, where Gloria resided on her days off. I knew little but was compelled to call. Connecting with a policeman, I told him about my father, the abuse I had been through and the strange disappearance of Gloria. I told him about my father's talk with the policeman at the door and my belief he was lying. Unprepared, I said on the phone that day, "I believe my father killed her."

I wanted to deny what was flowing out of my mouth, but I kept talking. He listened, then added, "We currently have a case where children from another family remembered their father killing their maid." Then, he added, "Back in 1963, live-in nannies went missing who came from other parts of the world. And black women from the South were rarely investigated."

This was too close to home for me. We lived in Merrick, Long Island, and had a live-in black woman from the South who went missing in 1963. It was conceivable to me that he got away with it back then. I kept asking myself, could this be true? Doubting, yet simultaneously knowing that I had witnessed something awful.

I still could not listen to the tape. I was terrified of the truth. Although I wanted desperately to remember, I realized that pushing the envelope was not in my best interest—not yet. It was all too much. I was slowly losing my ability to work, and after much debating with myself and the support of John, I gave up my part-time practice in 1992. My clients knew I was in recovery from sexual abuse and that I had had three miscarriages. I simply needed to rest and put my focus entirely on me. I felt as if I were abandoning ship as I told everyone I worked with that I was closing my practice.

After my first miscarriage, I was fearful that I might not be able to work during a pregnancy due to my age when another occurred. We bought a disability policy to put in place in case I became pregnant, and a complication arose. I never imagined that my disability would be due to PTSD and that I would have to give up my practice due to abuse recovery I was undergoing. I was inundated with memories, barely getting out of bed, hardly sleeping, fearful, anxious and depressed. I resisted any medication since I was in recovery. My addiction to painkillers was doctor prescribed. It was not another door I wanted to open. It was all too much.

CHAPTER FOURTEEN

The Reality of the Searing Knife Pain

*Reconnecting with
the hidden parts of myself
became my full-time job.*

IN OCTOBER OF 1992, I walked through the doors of an abuse recovery treatment facility in Los Angeles. It had a wing dedicated to sexual abuse recovery. It was a good decision, and I was grateful to be in a safe environment to do the work that needed to be done.

While hospitalized, I had an idea to use art as a tool as I did memory and inner child work. A memory surfaced of being young, sitting at a large table in my basement and surrounded by all types of art tools. I kept visualizing this table and was drawn to do finger painting on large poster board paper.

In my free time in the evening, I frantically threw paint on paper and let my hands roam freely as I expressed my memories. There was never any plan as to what I would create. I let the freedom of expression of my body flow through my fingers. I trusted what I needed to let out. Afterward, I wrote about each painting and went over it with my therapist.

Opening myself to art, memories were triggered of my father prying my legs open to have sex, insisting, "You are at the proper age for this." I was 12 then and remembered his warning to me when I was younger that he would do this to me at a later age.

Now was the time. Although I had already had pieces of memory, the full experience of it blasted in. My physical body screamed with pain. I was terrified and filled with shame. My young mind stepped in. *Little Lori, I'll take over. Let's go on a beautiful magic carpet ride—up, up and away from your body and high into the sky.*

My pain, my suffering, my shame, and my terror went unnoticed.

To move through the searing knife-like pain, I stood up, while I finger painted using my whole body while frantically moving until I could do no more for the night. The movement was freeing—leaving me thoroughly exhausted when I was finished.

Three finger paintings of dissociation on magic carpet rides through the sky.

He justified his actions. "A girl should be taught by her father."
He assured me, "I am the best person to do this. Someday you
will appreciate my being the teacher. After all, it was going to
hurt in the beginning so why not now?"

I heard him clearly say this to me, my protests unheard … his
wants and needs always came first.

So, my pain, my suffering, my shame, and my terror went
unnoticed. And my crying, begging, pleading did not matter.
Only his sick need for power and domination was the priority.

In the hospital, I remembered a phone conversation with my
mother while at my friend Linda's house. I was 16, had terrible
hay fever, and was furious at her. She called since I left our
house in a rage, wanting me to come home, but I refused,
saying, "I am staying at Linda's house for the weekend." And
then I added, "I hate my father and won't come home."

I was enraged when she asked, "What are you so angry at?"

"Why are you asking? You don't want to know," I responded.

She kept trying to get me to talk. I couldn't, and I hung up
on her, hating myself at the same
time.

**I will not come home if
you do not leave me alone.**

A few weeks later, while still in
the hospital, I remembered him telling me he wanted anal sex
and my outrage. I was angrier than I had ever remembered
and stood up to him in a way I had never done. "I will not come
home if you do not leave me alone," spilled out of my mouth.

The sexual abuse stopped. What I didn't know at the time was that he had a new target for his sexual abuse: my little brother, who was 10 years younger. In the hospital, I remembered waking one night to go to the bathroom, noticing my father's feet hanging over my brother's bed—the same bed I had at his age.

This realization that he was abusing my brother was devastating. I felt responsible since he was so much younger.

Pieces of memories opened as I let in this reality. I had tremendous guilt at getting married at 21, leaving him alone with my parents. Whenever I visited, the guilt surfaced when I left him behind. But in my amnesia, I never knew why this was so bothersome, just that it was.

I was overwhelmed with survivor guilt at leaving my brother with my father's sexual sickness. I had to work on forgiving myself since I did not have the power to stop him. I felt murderous rage at both my mother for not protecting us and my father for his sickness that had always been expressed toward me. Imploding rather than exploding, I let myself rage on.

> **For the first time, I realized that "killing myself" was not the answer.**

For the first time, I realized that "killing myself" was not the answer. Although I believed I had wanted to die when suicidal, I only wanted the pain to stop. I wanted to live, and I promised myself that I would no longer hurt myself because of his years of abuse. That meant I truly had to learn to love myself.

I stayed in the hospital for three months. I was overwhelmed with grief and rage, going back and forth between directing the rage at me versus outwardly toward my father and mother.

Some days passed where I could not get out of bed.

Some days, I sobbed uncontrollably with all that I had lost, including my virginity, and my loss of innocence as a child.

Remembering the feeling that the morning daylight created … a spotlight on my father's behavior the night before and how I had to hide this from my mother put my humiliation into overload.

It was a revelation that I had nothing to be ashamed about. I did not do "this" to me … my father did it. I was truly a victim of his sickness with no choice whatsoever, even as a teenager. I was terrified of him and what he might do to me.

Visualizations of rescuing and creating a safe place for my little girl became part of my daily experience. In the hospital, I would close my eyes and tightly hold a pillow. I would imagine I was holding myself at different ages. The recovering Adult Lori embraced the abused Little Girl Lori. I needed to love myself, starting with the little me in order to nurture me back to health.

The little girl Lori wrote to the adult Lori self-revealing letters that talked about her abuse, the dissociation and other abilities she had buried deep inside. For instance, I started writing with my right hand, remembering that I did as a child even though I'm left-handed. I wrote daily, switching from one hand to the other. This was new. I have always been able to do other things in both hands, but writing script with both was different. My finger painting had triggered my ability to express myself. Poetry began to flow when I wrote with my right hand.

I was bursting with a creative ability that I had turned my back on at age twelve. Memories of taking oil painting classes and doing still lifes and how much I loved to paint materialized. The joy of writing creative essays in elementary school and submitting them to the school paper emerged. Up until this point in my recovery, I had no access to these creative abilities. Yet, they were there, waiting to come out. I was grateful to reconnect to myself and slowly recover all that I had lost along the way.

I realized that connecting to the bad enabled my creativity to blossom. Likening myself to a house with unexplored hallways and unopened rooms, a new me was surfacing. While in dissociation, I created many locked doors. Behind each contained trauma, memories that had been frozen in time with its images, sounds, smells, and feelings stored exactly how they had happened. Each time I opened the door to a room, I discovered pieces of myself that broke apart and were left behind in the trauma.

The age of twelve was a pivotal point in my life. Up until then, I was involved in art. My father's increasing abuse overwhelmed my senses. No wonder I shut down by turning myself off to close my body off from overwhelming abuse sensations. It helped me to survive. But with the turnoff, I lost my creative passion. Using all my energy to deaden myself resulted in tragic consequences—from developing eating disorders and using drugs to deadening any pleasure.

Prior to this hospitalization, I spent years helping other people and loved doing this through my practice, something I was also mourning as I closed it down. It was a difficult decision, but I knew my focus had to be on only me at this time. The nightmares, memories, and flashbacks I was bombarded with all involved terror. Reconnecting with the hidden parts of myself became my full-time job.

CHAPTER FIFTEEN

The Scream

I wanted to feel alive,
passionate and joyful,
all that I lost as a child.

WHEN I GOT OUT OF THE HOSPITAL, I immediately contacted
Lakeside Elementary School where I was a student through
the sixth grade. Reaching the school's secretary, I explained to
her that I was recovering from abuse and part of the recovery
process was backtracking. Asking if she knew if the school had
records dating back to when I was a student, the years from
1955 to 1962, she responded that she would check.

To my surprise, I received records from that time. What struck
me was the statement: *Talented in music and art.* It was written
by my sixth-grade teacher, a teacher that I connected with.
As a student, I loved to be in his classroom. Although I was
remembering my artistic abilities, it was shocking to see this
written about me. Talents that have been buried in the dark
cloud of my childhood … and ones that I had never identified
within myself.

I reached out to my former teacher. To my surprise, he
remembered me and revealed that I had created large murals
for his classroom. Me? Then he said what he'd written on my
report card: "You were talented." When I revealed what I had

MARKS

In the space after each subject please record a mark that would best represent a final mark, if such a mark were being given at this time.

English _____ 5+

Citizenship Education _____ 1=

Science _____ 5 +

Mathematics _____ 5

COMMENTS

Comments are included because teachers observe personal behavior, personality traits, abilities and talents, mental and physical handicaps, unusual home conditions and other factors that key importance and yet cannot be obtained from other responses. Please use this space for your comsign your name on the line provided.

Produces fine projects. Talented on art and music.

Member of a regular reading group

Signed *Mr. O. P. x*

Remarks made by my 6th grade teacher Mr. Peti.

been going through, he said, "That doesn't surprise me. You were flirtatious in a way that was not age appropriate."

He had known something was wrong with me!

"In 1962, sexual abuse was not recognized, nor talked about … or reported," he added. "You did come to mind years later when it was." He told me that when he thought about the symptoms I had presented, he believed I had been abused. It was another 30 years before the mandatory reporting was required in all 50 states under the Child Abuse Prevention and Treatment Act (CAPTA). Thirty-plus years!

No wonder I felt safe with him when I was young. I now remembered having a "crush" on him, silently wishing he was my father.

I was on a quest, wanting to know who the "student" Lori was. When I received copies of my junior and senior high school records, I discovered what I wanted to do when I was older. I wrote as a child: *Help people.* The social services field was a magnet, and on an aptitude test, it was the category in which I scored the highest. Interestingly, I became a Licensed Clinical Social Worker, which I always believed was a natural choice.

The process of feeding my soul was paramount; the type of art I produced was not.

After my conversation with him, I decided to take a drawing class. During the first class, we were asked to draw a hand holding a pencil. It was as if I were watching myself draw; I was amazed at my ability. The teacher held up my drawing as she went around the class. After class, I talked with her and explained I was in abuse recovery and was rediscovering my artistic ability.

She was surprised to learn that I stopped doing any art between the ages of 12 and 13. It was as if I had been drawing my whole life. My ability to do this was frozen in time as well as the knowledge of my abuse.

I was tired of grieving ... and ready to live.

Daily, I was drawing. When I finished this class, I went on to learn how to paint. I found a teacher who would help me discover my own style. I participated in a private group class and learned how to use charcoal and paint with oils and acrylics. I continued for many years and loved it.

Arts Anonymous caught my attention, and I joined its 12-step program. Winning a special award for student photographers at the Del Mar Fair encouraged me to explore my creativity. What else could I do?

Opening the creative door that had been shut at 13 for survival had consequences. My artistic expression brought forth the extensive abuse I experienced in a visual, in-my-face format. Fear arose, causing me to back off and want to shut down.

Arts Anonymous focused on my avoidance, my perfectionism, feeling I am not good enough, my fear of failure, my fear of success, and my fear of attention. The goal in ARTS is to "achieve an active, abundant, full and robust life focused on our creativity." I met people who were practicing their art. I wanted the freedom to express myself in any way that felt important. I sought teachers to help keep me active and inspire me. Individuals were coming into my life who understood my recovery from sexual abuse and my fears of opening to a creative expression that had been dormant for two decades.

My Emerging Scream remembering age 12 and 13

I was grateful for their support. The process of feeding my soul was paramount; the type and style of art I produced was not. I wanted to feel alive, passionate and joyful, all that I lost as a child. I was tired of grieving … and ready to live.

The Horror of remembering age 12 and 13

Self Portrait of Myself as a Teenager

My Invisible Wall of Secrecy

CHAPTER SIXTEEN

Age 13 — My Black Hole

I See What You Did Remembering Gloria

What happened to Gloria?
Why did she leave?

IT WAS 1991, and I had just had my third heart-wrenching miscarriage. Memories were resurfacing and our live-in nanny Gloria entered my mind. When I was 13, she just disappeared. Here one day and gone the next. While in the hospital and afterward from 1992-1993, more was revealed.

During one of my painting classes, I painted myself, younger, with my left hand covering my left eye, and an image showing in my right eye.

Months later, I was driving at night along the shore and by accident turned down a very dark road surrounded by tall reeds. FoPo wasn't with me, which was unusual due to my continual living-in-terror life.

While on this road, I panicked. The curtain opens; I'm in a flashback.

> I'm 13 and can't breathe. I felt trapped as though I would never get out. Confusion permeates me. I'm spooked. Where am I? Why am I here? I'm desperate to get away. I'm engulfed in a foggy darkness and gripped by evil. I know that I am witnessing a horror I could not yet see. I screamed and broke down in gulping sobs. Frozen, I could not get myself out of this veil of darkness.

Finally, I calmed down through breathing—a window begins to open.

The curtain closes. No longer am I 13. I'm now 42 with my hands on the steering wheel of my car. The road ahead is dark, yet no longer horrifying. I know I am experiencing my emotions being in control. But why? And why am I recalling Gloria now?

I felt the reality of the swinging pendulum about to get me.

I don't remember driving home.

Entering my home, I was terrified and shaking. Beginning to pace and frightened to look out my windows, I felt my life was in danger. I called my confidant and my survivor buddy Madelyn, and in a quivering voice I blurted out, "I witnessed something terrible."

That was how flashbacks occurred, pieces of information, a little at a time. My life had become a series of cliff-hangers woven around the flashbacks, as if I was watching a scene in a horror movie when suddenly the power shuts down. When will it turn back on? The waiting becomes intolerable, not knowing when the show will resume—only that it will in time. I'm left hanging in suspense and feeling absolute powerlessness knowing no amount of swimming upstream will work. I must let go of my internal struggle, my need to know what I am not ready to know, love myself, believing it will come when I am ready, practicing what I had already learned.

I went through a period of feeling queasy and unable to watch movies with violence using knives. I felt as though I was under the knife about to be sliced like I did in my teens when Allen Poe's short story *The Pit and the Pendulum* surfaced. I felt the reality of the swinging pendulum about to get me. As soon as

I saw a scene with a knife, I curled up with a need to protect myself. I felt the knife touching my skin as though I was being warned:

Don't see.

Don't remember.

Don't tell.

My father's threats.

I was living once again in my SILENT SCREAM.

My Scream, with my father lurking.

Memories came in stages. Months later while taking a bath, the curtain opens.

> It's night, and I see my father come up behind Gloria while I am talking with her. He swings a large piece of wood at her head, and I see her startled eyes, her disbelieving that "this" is happening. The sound of the wood slamming her head and her slumping to the sand leaves me in shock, unable to move, unable to breathe.

The curtain closes. Back in my bathtub, I know that he murdered her. I stiffen, stunned, and too afraid to move. *Breathe, Lori,* I tell myself. *You need to bring life back into yourself.*

By the time John came home, I was sitting on my couch with a vacant stare, barely able to talk. "Lori, you are scaring me … you look like you witnessed a murder," he said.

I think my father killed our nanny.

In a detached flat voice, I respond, "I know my father murdered Gloria." I felt glued to the couch, unable to move. "I need time to sit and absorb this."

Soon, disbelief followed. How could I have kept this from myself for so many years? Once again, I went back and forth believing and disbelieving. Could this be real? It was the same feeling as when I first remembered his sexual abuse. Then I recalled my flashbacks: my absolute terror; my vision of being 13 and within a black hole; of hearing my father telling the police at our front door that he has not seen her; of knowing in that moment, he was lying; and my call to the detective saying, "I think my father killed our nanny." Then there is my dissociation and my elimination of my artistic abilities. Continually cycling through these thoughts, I always came back to "I know this happened. I am not crazy."

When I was hospitalized, I gave the tape of my previous Doriden session to my assigned psychiatrist. I still could not remember the session and was too afraid to listen to the recording. I knew I was describing a scene on our boat that I witnessed involving Gloria. Agreeing that it was too soon for me to listen, he believed the session was properly conducted by the psychologist. He did say that it included a disturbing and detailed description of what occurred. He said, "It is awful."

The tape, along with journals of my incest recovery was stored in my garage with the thought that I would listen to it when I was ready. It wasn't meant to be. When I had the garage cleaned, the tape was thrown out along with various notebooks I hadn't intended to discard. At first, I was really upset, but I soon practiced what I learned in recovery. I let go knowing I suffered enough. I accepted that I was not supposed to listen to that tape.

**I know this happened.
I am not crazy.**

Slowly, I pieced together what happened to Gloria.

> My mother is out and my father took her and me out on our boat on Gloria's night off. Gloria was scared on the boat but displayed the fear in a comical way, my laughing with her, my father reassuring her all would be okay. We pulled into a secluded beach with tall reeds growing in the outlying area. I can see me standing next to a fire he built. I can't see anyone else with me. I see him in the distance arguing with Gloria. She returns and stands next to the fire to warm up. In

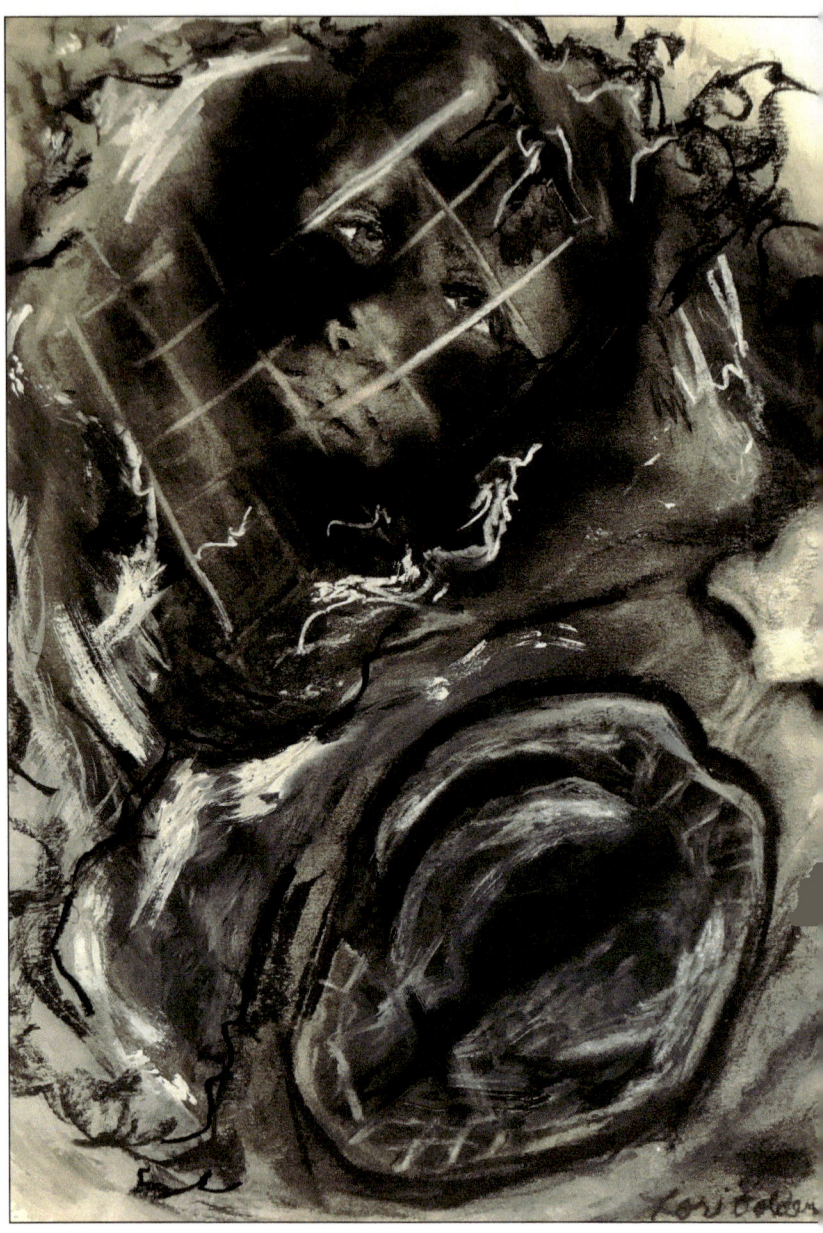

Imprisoned in Horror

a nervous voice, she says, "Your father's really angry with me."

I see him come back gripping a large piece of firewood in his hand. I'm talking and looking at Gloria, but my attention is on him as he comes up behind her, swings the wood, and hits her on the head. I see her stunned look, the startled eyes, her slumping to the sand as he hits her again—and then, my shock.

In a furious tone, he is saying to me, "I got her pregnant, and she threatened to tell your mother. And then, almost as an aside, "I couldn't let that happen. Your mother can never find out ... I will lose everything."

Repeatedly, he was justifying his need to kill her. Hearing his disembodied voice combined with my looking through a hazy fog not able to see what I saw ... not to know what I knew ... and not to feel what I felt ... I had to run from the truth. I survived, deadening life within myself. My creative energy and my natural life force were shut down. It was a great sacrifice.

Seemingly out of nowhere, Gloria's image came to me, years before this memory, and I began to wonder about her. Where did she go? When I was still speaking with my mother early in my abuse recovery, I asked her, "What happened to Gloria? Why did she leave us?"

Surprisingly, my mother got angry. "Why are you asking about her?"

I was taken off guard, not expecting her reaction. I hesitated, suddenly careful, and said, "I don't know. I was just thinking about her."

"That's odd," she replied. Then she added that Gloria locked herself in her room with my brother, saying she had a knife and would hurt him. When I questioned her further, she rebuffed me, saying, "She was crazy. I fired her after that."

I knew it wasn't true. She was lying. The explanation she gave did not make sense, but I knew not to question her further. A few years later, the memory of standing on the stairs listening to my father lie to the police surfaced along with hearing my mother question him about her disappearance. My father's outright lie: that he hadn't seen Gloria for some time … and how it was so strange that she would leave her clothes behind. After the police left, I remember hearing my parents arguing. I don't think my mother believed him.

Although I was not able to recall the details of the boat scene, I knew we were out in the ocean afterward with Gloria's body. *He was going to discard it.* I know the boat scene was about him dissecting her. I did not have to remember every gory detail.

My father was a sick man, and I knew he was capable of violence.

I worked with a psychiatrist specializing in hypnosis prior to my hospitalization trying to recall my life at age 13, the black hole. During one of our sessions, I smelled the sickening odor of formaldehyde. Afterward, I was grocery shopping and saw a jar of gefilte fish since it was a Jewish holiday. The curtain suddenly opens, and I gasp.

Within the jar, a body part preserved in Formaldehyde emerges. I was unable to breathe, trying
to make sense of what I was seeing. Confused,
I was light-headed and frozen in place.

The curtain closes. Remembering to breathe, I abandoned my cart and ran from the store.

I went into the hospital seeking a safe place to continue my therapy. I learned in my recovery that I did not need every detail to validate my truth. What I was supposed to remember, I recalled in order to move forward. I stopped trying to access memories in 1993. Instead, I painted, played music, and began to write children's songs. All that mattered was feeling my aliveness, expressing myself without holding back. I was now ready for the next chapter of my life to begin: adoption.

CHAPTER SEVENTEEN

The Gift
of Jason

Loss brings wonderful gifts
if I move through the grief
and let go.

AFTER MY FIRST MISCARRIAGE, I turned the baby's room
into my piano room in my grief. Not knowing when or if I
would get pregnant again, I felt learning to play would help
me heal a deep longing inside of myself. The room became
my special safe place to grieve, nurture myself, heal and grow.

After I discovered my love of painting, and that I had painted
as a child, I hired someone to build a painting shed in my backyard. A place I could be as messy as I needed to be and free
to paint whatever I needed to with no holding back. It was
another safe place that was created to continue in my healing
journey.

I wanted to be a mom; healing was my number one priority.
I knew that I could not live in my abuse and under my father's
abusive impact any longer. It was time for the next chapter of
my life. I was ready to move on … to let go.

John and I met with an adoption lawyer in Los Angeles to
sign the paperwork and we moved forward in the process. I was
now 45.

Christmas Eve 1994 is embedded solidly within me. John and I were surrounded by many friends from our recovery groups. Over dinner, I lit three candles to honor our three miscarriages one last time saying, "I am ready to let go." I wanted my heart to be completely open to love my child who was on his or her way.

Two hours later, we got *the phone call* from our lawyer. "We located a birth mom about to give birth in Hemet, California. Can you both go and meet her tomorrow?" It was a night I will always remember.

Once again, I learned the lesson of *letting go*. Every time I let go in my recovery, I opened to what was supposed to happen next in my life.

It was ten days that felt endless. We spent Christmas Day and the following four days with the birth mother who went into labor on December 29th, the day my son Jason was born. I was in the delivery room throughout to witness his incredible birth. I will always be grateful to her for the gift of my son.

Marveling at what had happened, we took Jason home … and then held our breath for the next ten days. Ten long days waiting to hear if the birth mother would change her mind … ten long days to know if the court would finalize the adoption.

My lawyer helped change the waiting period from six months to ten days when we started the process. I fell in love immediately and could not have imagined waiting six months. It was ten days that felt endless.

John went to court while I stayed home with Jason to wait to see if the adoption was finalized. Madelyn who accompanied

A drawing I did right after the adoption was finalized.

me throughout my recovery, sat with me while I waited. We both cried with relief when I got the call from our attorney. He simply said, "Congratulations." And Jason was officially our child.

After six years of grieving multiple miscarriages, waiting, worrying, suffering and wondering when, and if, I would have a child, my dream came true. This process taught me an invaluable lesson. Loss brings wonderful gifts if I move through the grief and let go. Only then can I leave room for new possibilities. I now know if I am truly meant to have something in my life, I will … if I am willing to focus my heartfelt attention on it.

I realized that the pain of miscarrying and loss was necessary for Jason to come into my life, a life I can't imagine without him.

CHAPTER EIGHTEEN

Losses and Gains

I worked hard on my codependency
throughout my recovery.

THE YEARS 1994–1997 delivered significant changes for all of us. I continued my painting and music lessons. I wrote children's songs for Jason; one song he loved was "Shadow Friends." One night while feeding Jason I looked at shadows on the wall, realizing I no longer saw them as scary and imagined turning them into friends and joyful images. Something that I had never learned as a child.

I began painting and drawing images that reflected who I had become—not about my abuse. Although I was tired from the past seven years, I found my inner strength.

Relationships Change

Unfortunately, my growth resulted in John and I growing apart. Our marriage ended in divorce. When I met him in early recovery, a frightened Little Girl Lori was ever present. As I worked on myself and my sexual abuse, my needs changed, and I changed.

After adopting Jason, I realized that John was not willing to continue to commit to recovery in ways that were important to me. I felt I was the captain of a ship that was sinking, and my growing concerns about our drifting apart were falling on deaf ears. I was tired of pushing to get my needs met. I wanted

Shadow Friends

Shadow friends on the wall
Some are big and some are small
Close your eyes they go away
But don't go far they want to play

Look and see
Open wide
They're here for you
No need to hide
They come at night
When lights are out
They love to dance
And move about

Lie in bed and make believe
Your shadows are the birds and trees
Think of all the things you love
A friend, a dog, a cat, a dove
Your favorite toy
A girl or boy
Your teddy bear
Birds in the air

Don't be afraid
You're not alone
Your shadow friends really care

They come at night when
Lights are out they love to
Dance and move about
On the ceiling on the wall
Some are big and some are small

Squiggly lines, circles too
Square and dots all for you
Just lie in bed and make believe
Your shadows are the birds
and trees

Think of all the things you love
A friend, a dog, a cat, a dove
Your favorite toy
A girl or boy
Your teddy bear
Birds in the air

Don't be afraid
You're not alone
Your shadow friends
Live in your home

to be heard and responded to out of his own willingness to do this without my prompting and initiating any step forward.

I worked hard on my codependency throughout my recovery. Driven by fear, I focused on John's moods, his feelings, and trying to assess what he needed. My belief was that if he got what he needed, I would get what I needed, and I would be safe. My efforts were unproductive—something I didn't see or understand until further along in my own recovery. The codependency on John grew out of survival skills learned from focusing on my father, believing if I knew something about him, I could keep myself safe. That never worked. Gradually, I learned to keep the focus on myself and my feelings, and not John's … my needs, not his. I gave up pushing and wanting him to be different.

When I stopped using food to numb myself, I saw our differences clearly. I saw how I tried to impose my way of doing things rather than sit back to see what he was willing to do. I was afraid if I did this, I would not get what I needed. I wanted him to initiate a conversation, tell me how he felt, tell me what he needed. John needed much less interaction than I did. Slowly, we both came to terms with our incompatibility. I had to stop doing what I did in order to see clearly that our needs were different. We both did. They were neither good or bad … just different.

I grew and grew up.

The New Me

Learning how to keep the focus on myself helped me to come to terms with our lack of connection and intimacy. I changed my behavior. I stopped pulling. I was no longer willing to lie

My Gift of Strength My Wisdom, My Courage, My Strength

to myself. I let go of the belief that I was not enough without a man by my side. I got into this relationship out of my fear of being alone, a self-centered motive.

There is a saying that until you learn to love yourself, you cannot love another. I did not know who I was when I got into recovery and met John. I was on a spiral of self-destruction and filled with self-hatred. I was a needy little girl, not a grown woman. I had blind spots in my choices of men, not seeing what I needed to see, always going into confusion when in fact my intuition was spot-on. When I looked back on all my relationships, I ignored warning signs, just to be in a relationship and not alone. If I could not trust myself, my inner voice, then how could I expect to get my needs met? And—more importantly —to love freely.

I will always be grateful to John for the years we spent together. We helped each other in many ways through a very difficult time in both of our lives. He had always been someone I could call to ask for help, and continued to be someone I could call throughout Jason's growing-up years.

Several years after John and I separated, I met Jeff. When we met, I felt ready to have another man in my life. I trusted myself. I knew how to identify what I felt and was able to express my needs directly. I never had to guess with Jeff. He shared his thoughts, his feelings and his concerns and I did as well. We laughed a lot, and I loved his sense of humor. We had a lot in common. He was an excellent athlete, so we enjoyed sports together, and he was a gifted piano player. I loved listening to his improvising. His music was soothing and I never tired of it. Jeff was my soul mate.

We moved in together. Both his son and daughter would join us on weekends. We played games and had a lot of fun together. Jeff was always inventing games on the spur-of-the-moment and the kids loved it. While we were out, he would suddenly challenge them to do something, and if they did it, they would earn a quarter. He understood how to play with kids and how to motivate them. I loved this about him and valued this special quality.

We planned on getting married; it was not to be. In 2002, Jeff died suddenly. Taking Jason to his friend's house in the morning, I returned to wake Jeff. By the time I opened the door to our room, I could not believe what I was seeing and hearing. He was breathing erratically and appeared to be in a coma.

I was in a state of shock for quite some time.

911 was called. Jeff died on the way to the hospital. I was in complete shock. My friend Madelyn was now a nurse and immediately came to the hospital to be with me. The social worker helped me to call his children. John came over to help me tell Jason that Jeff had died. It was awful and so unfair. How could this have happened to us when all was so good?

The autopsy did not reveal a cause of death other than he aspirated in his sleep causing asphyxiation. I went over the autopsy report with his doctor who had seen him the day before his death. The doctor was shocked. As much as I wanted another reason for his death besides "he aspirated causing asphyxiation," I was not going to get one. My searching for answers helped me to postpone the feeling of his loss. When I let go, grieving set in.

I was in a state of shock for quite some time. I focused on Jason's needs and was grateful that I practiced living a day at a time in my recovery program. I reassured myself that I only had to live without him each day, one day at a time. I stayed away from thinking about a future without him, constantly bringing myself back to *the now*, to today. It was something I learned to do when I gave up drugs in 1987. In early recovery I was taught to only think about the next indicated thing I had to do to get through a day clean.

I learned to accept what was rather then wish it were different.

And, I had a wonderful son who had grown into an amazing young man. A son that I've held back no secrets from the journey I came through.

After Jeff died, I went back to work, creating my practice and helping others and staying connected with my support group. I focused on the next thing I had to do that day until I went to sleep. Future thinking was deferred.

Along with building my practice, Jason was my world. I had to help Jason cope with this sudden loss. We read children's books on death and spirituality, which was comforting to both of us. Death was a mystery to me, and I was seeking ways to understand it as well as to help him. We would look up in the sky and wonder if Jeff was up there. At night, we imagined Jeff listening while we told him what we did that day. We always included what we missed about him and something we were thankful for.

I was so grateful for the time I did get to spend with Jeff. There was nothing left unsaid. He knew I loved him, and I knew he loved me. Would I have wanted more? Of course. But I learned to accept what was, rather than wish it were different. This was a huge step for the new Lori.

I lived in myself with Jeff in a way I never had. I did not lose me when he died. It was something I had never experienced before. I knew I could go on and that grief would not kill me. I felt a profound loss, but my grief was for him, not the loss of my childhood. It was scary to walk through but not filled with monsters in the night. I found strength in myself that I gained throughout the previous years. I did not get stuck in feeling sorry for myself but instead, felt grateful for what I had.

The new Lori would survive and thrive. And she had her son at her side.

CHAPTER NINETEEN

My Life Going Forward

I did not need her
to admit to my father's abuse
or to validate my truth.

FOR MANY YEARS, I lived in the trenches of abuse and the strains of recovery. The work I had to do to find myself and move forward left me too emotionally exhausted to work with people. I needed to recuperate from many years of terror than my father, the ape, had created. I was not able to sponsor people in my recovery program because I did not trust my ability to be in a way that was needed. What I learned about me was that I had to be careful not to take on too much, to ease back into life … and breathe. Even though I loved working with people, I wondered if I could ever go back to my profession.

As he lived, Jeff's dying was a gift. It delivered the catalyst for me to begin my professional life once again. Beginning in 2003, I returned to my work, initially on a part-time basis because of the demand for concentrated focus. My work past was one where I worked despite being self-destructive. Others' needs were more important than my own, a result of codependency. Now, I am the most important. I've learned to respond to my needs first; otherwise, I cannot effectively teach others. Today, I have self-respect and love for myself—a gift from Jeff.

I have always valued working with others. I know it is what I am supposed to do. My work is who I have become, an outgrowth of sexual abuse. I lived in trauma and addiction, and now I live in recovery in body, mind, and spirit. I am my work, dedicated to helping others on their journey to heal.

Reuniting with My Mother

It had been sixteen years since I had met with my mother. I was not sure about what I wanted except to feel my own strength and to introduce Jason since he wanted to meet her. What I was sure about was that I did not need her to admit to my father's abuse or to validate my truth.

I knew that I would no longer self-destruct because of any rage toward her for not protecting me, for not stopping it. My anger was in the past. Nor did I care if she believed he sexually abused me. I did not want to discuss the past because there was nothing that I wanted from her. *I knew the truth—my truth.* I also knew from my sister that she did not pursue her own sexual abuse recovery within the family. Without her own self-exploration in this, I did not want to revisit it.

I'm thankful that Jason never encountered my father, whose death occurred before he was born. He had asked early on about my mother and father. When Jason was younger, I explained my relationship with my parents **Only I must see my truth.** through children's books on abuse. I ordered a program that used puppets to talk about difficult subjects, particularly good and bad touching. We read about adoption as well so he would slowly understand these challenging and difficult subjects. He always asked questions, and I tried to answer simply and honestly.

My niece and nephews benefitted from having my mother in their lives. She was good for them, and I wanted Jason to meet her and decide for himself. When Jason was nine, my mother and I met again. She and her husband came to my house to meet Jason for the first time.

He liked her immediately. She was warm and engaging and knew how to make him feel comfortable. My friends had always liked my mother, and so did kids and counselors at our day camp where she was the head counselor for years. She was someone people confided in.

When I was a child, I had a wall around me and was guarded in her presence. She lived in denial and chose not to see what was really going on in our house. I did not know what our relationship would be like now, except that I was different and no longer fearful. And I was watchful for Jason's sake.

My mother has been in my life again since the mid-2000s and is now in her mid-nineties. I am glad we reunited. She and her husband turned Jason and me onto golf. We have dinners and spend holidays and birthdays together. Family comes out to visit us in California, which Jason and I enjoy. I can talk honestly with my sister and brother, who both understand and know that my father abused them as well as me.

I always believed you about your father.

When I told her I was writing my story, she said, "Good for you." She added, "I always believed you about your father." We discussed my calling the Child Protective Services and her claiming, "Your father was a good father." She explained that she lied to CPS because of pressure from others, believing my sister's kids would be taken away if it was discovered that my father was entering their bathroom when they bathed. I didn't like it nor did I support it, but I understood it.

Blaming is my mother's way of not taking responsibility for her own actions and choices. I did not confront this since I learned years ago not to give away my energy "trying" to get her to see—one of my greatest gifts in my recovery. *Only I must see my truth.* Others seeing it doesn't make it more true. I am grateful to have learned powerlessness. I no longer struggle in ways that are not necessary.

As with all children, I am a combination of my mother and father. I hated that I could be anything like them. For years, I did not want to be like them or have any association with them. And for years, I did not want to see their special qualities. I've learned that people are not black and white but different shades of color. I chose not to live in their sickness and denial, but I can appreciate the good attributes that they possess. I have my father's ability to master whatever I put my mind to, his creativity, his athletic ability and his interest in learning new hobbies. And I have my mother's desire to help others, her engaging ability, her agelessness, and her love of adventure. Both are intelligent people. I'm thankful that I am, too.

They told me they loved me throughout my growing-up years. Their type of love was confusing and never touched my soul where I was gravely wounded. Over the years, I learned that love must feel safe for me. The only way it can is through honesty and transparency. I cannot trust the depth of anyone's proclaimed love without it. Therefore, my relationship with my mother is limited, and I accept this limitation. I apply this to other people as well. I learned how to stop trying to get more when it led to my suffering—another gift in my recovery.

The childhood sexual abuse I endured for eleven years created a house of lies that lived for decades, long after the sexual abuse had stopped. It was brutal, debilitating, and dominoed to my sister and brother who were targeted as well. At times, I didn't think I would survive. I did, with help.

I now know that it can end. *My House of Lies* is a revelation of horror I went through that shadowed my life long into my adult years. And it's a promise … a promise to be there for others; to help them through the steps to recovering and recovery; and to encourage others to see and embrace their truth.

CHAPTER TWENTY

Why Don't Children Tell?

I did not even have the words
to describe what was happening.

IT'S AN IMPORTANT QUESTION TO ASK. And the answer is not complicated: Adults are powerful, and children are helpless. My father threatened me in many ways *not to tell*. "It's our secret." Repeatedly, he put a finger to his lips and the sound, *SHUSH*.

Like so many survivors, I lived in terror, shame, confusion, and dissociation as well as chronic lack of sleep. Sleep deprivation is a form of torture. It is used as a tactic to break prisoners down. Being a child of sexual abuse, I was held hostage and imprisoned by my father's sick cravings. All I wanted to do was sleep. My needs did not matter. He was a sex addict. I knew when he had that "sex look" in his eyes that nothing I said or did would matter. So, I learned to get away, to survive, by dissociating from my body. My mind took me to a different place when every assault occurred, and I stayed silent. *SHUSH*.

Make believe is a form of survival.

Children learn how to do this. It's how they survive. They detach from their bodies. They do it so well that they can deny their reality.

In my case, I lived in a state of amnesia, knowing something was happening, feeling dirty, sleep deprived, and in a state of confusion thinking I must have had a bad dream. Why am I so tired? In addition, I created an imaginary ape that I believed was the source of my terror—not my father. Then when I got older, it was an imaginary man that lived in the attic that was going to get me. Again, I never thought it was my father. Children can live in a make-believe world but learn the difference between real and unreal. Survivors of childhood sexual abuse don't. Make-believe is a form of survival.

Inside my room, I was isolated and cut off from the rest of my family. The dark helped to hide the monster and what was happening within my four walls. I was alone. There was no one to help; no one to witness what occurred; no one to reach out to … only me. And I did not even have the words to describe what was happening.

I must be bad.

Children shouldn't be having sex of any kind. They don't have the ability to describe overstimulation. It shorts out their brains and disrupts thinking. Too much to process at once, coupled with lack of vocabulary, are why children stay silent. It is too complicated for them.

Everyone in the family stays silent for that matter. No one addresses the behaviors that are sexualized outside of the bedroom. There is always evidence in families, but often the non-abusing parent doesn't address it. There are many reasons for this but suffice it to say they live in denial. They become complicit and at times co-conspirators with their spouse or partner.

I lived in a constant state of guilt around my mother. "Daddy" told me that he only did these special things with me and

Mommy wouldn't like that he preferred me over her. My guilt was consuming. I hated myself because there was no one to be angry at. If no one is accepting responsibility, then children take that to mean *I must be bad. I did something wrong … I am worthless. I am unlovable.*

These negative beliefs are created out of the adult's silence about what is happening. It leads to secrecy and shame. Self-hatred turns inward and leads to self-destructive behavior. Children create a type of war zone with themselves, fighting within, not without. They become the battleground, bombarded with demands by the perpetrator.

Many survivors of childhood sexual abuse reveal that when they did reach out for "help," they were not believed. They were challenged. And they were often told, "He wouldn't do that." Yes, he did.

They are telling you someone did something to them.

If children are saying that an adult is or was inappropriate, behaving sexually in some way, then believe them. They are telling the truth. How would any child under seven know about such behavior in the first place? If they are describing something that is not age appropriate, adults must listen and take it seriously. Do not blame it on TV or video games. Do not dismiss this as too much information on the internet. *They are telling you someone did something to them.*

Not paying attention becomes a violation of trust that leads to fear and further mistrust if not followed up. Investigate. Pay attention. Look, see, and don't hide. Seek help.

Commitment to Heal

Healing is a conscious decision. If you have been thinking that some form of sexual abuse occurred in your past when you were a child, then take it seriously. You are not sick, crazy, or have a wild imagination. Where there is smoke, there is fire. If you are in self-doubt, begin by listening to yourself and seeking information to learn more. It may have happened once, it may have been from an adult outside the family, it may be someone you don't know, or it could be someone close. If you are questioning something, then find answers for yourself. No one else will but you. Stop your excuses and take yourself seriously.

Survivors of childhood abuse often say, "It was in the past. I don't want to deal with it." My years of abuse carried long into my adulthood. The work I do now with patients around sexual trauma and addictions was seeded in childhood long ago.

It is not in the past.
It is alive in the present.

Your past lives in your choices. It lives in your decisions, your nightmares, your self-destructive behaviors, your hypervigilance, your relationships and in your sexuality. It silently guides you in your behavior today as an adult.

If you have flashbacks (like I did) or bits and pieces that something is just not right, try telling another person that you have these thoughts of something happening to you as a child. Or, something happening as an adult. Can you do this? What stops you?

It's time for you to address it. You can write down your reasons for not telling. Then you can find information about other survivors' reasons for not telling. It helps to see your thoughts verbalized by others. Know you are not alone.

When survivors say they remember, it's common for them to think they do not need further healing. But they do. Is that you? All inappropriate, sexualized behavior is shocking to the system when it occurs. Children freeze, have trouble breathing, and become confused. They don't tell because they don't understand what has happened or what's creating their behavior. It also occurs in adults who experienced sexual abuse of any sort, including rape when it hasn't been disclosed.

It means you are no longer alone.

No matter what the age or the degree of the sexual abuse, something happens to your body. Even a sexualized look from an adult can lead to "creepy" feelings that you experience in your body. If you kept silent, then the secrecy creates a wall around you in some way and separates you from others. "The tell" is necessary. You now have let someone into that walled-off space. It means you are no longer alone.

If you don't tell, then you live in secrecy and stay connected to your abuser. Telling for me meant I was no longer alone behind the closed door in the dark with my father. It allowed me to believe that what happened was real. I was no longer a secret to myself and others.

This is the beginning of healing. Take this first step. There are online programs as well as face-to-face programs that deal with sexual abuse. A variety of groups exist, such as:

- Survivors of Incest Anonymous at *www.SIAWSO.org*,

- Help for Adult Victims of Child Abuse at *HAVOCA.org*, or

- RAINN, the anti-sexual violence organization at *RAINN.org*.

Books, such as the *Courage to Heal* by Ellen Bass and Laura Davis as well the *Courage to Heal Workbook* by Laura Davis and *Beyond Betrayal* by Richard Gartner for boyhood sexual abuse.

If you can't afford outside help, there are many books and resources at your local library.

Begin by learning more about sexual abuse.

Reaching Out

If you never reached out to someone to tell, I know how frightening it can be. For me, I believed no one would care. I also believed the threats I was told as a child from my father not to tell. When I did "the tell," I lived in fear after I disclosed the abuse, but it was also incredibly relieving. My secrecy created shame and shame was awful to experience. Unfortunately, it is a necessary part of healing. It was the perpetrator that did the shameful behavior, not you.

Yes, you participated, but there was no choice. Everyone is ashamed that they "let" it happen, even adults. Blaming yourself is just a way to avoid all the feelings associated with sexual abuse. You need to understand what happened in that moment.

Violation of any sort is not okay. No one should touch or invade another's body without consent.

You don't have to live with this for the rest of your life. Whether you know it or not, you continue to live in fear today if you don't tell. A favorite expression is used within the 12-step programs: *You are only as sick as your secrets.* This has become a reminder I live by. I know how true it was for me and everyone I have talked to who has survived abuse and trauma whether as a child or adult.

Tell.
Release the secret.
Healing creates renewal.

CHAPTER TWENTY-ONE

My Story Is Your Story … from My Heart to Yours

The greatest gift I got
by remembering and in my abuse recovery
was learning to trust myself.

I WANT YOU TO REMEMBER that everything you experience on your healing journey you have already lived through as a child. The difference today is that you never have to endure the pain alone.

As I started to remember, I realized how alone I was in my abuse.

I couldn't cry out for help.

I couldn't tell anyone because
I felt I was to blame and feared the consequences.

This left me feeling deeply ashamed as well as having to live in secrecy. And I learned that secrecy separated me from people. It created a wall that I lived behind. It was scary to let anybody in because deep down, I believed I was dirty. Filthy. I carried the shame that belonged to the people who hurt me.

I want you to remember that you can never turn your back on the abuse you endured because you cannot run from yourself. You can't say it was in the past—because you live it every day in one way or another.

It's in the way you feel about yourself:

The beliefs you carry about yourself and others.

The way you are in relationships.

The way you protect yourself.

The fears and belief that you are unsafe.

The never-ending nighttime fears and nightmares.

The need to be hypervigilant.

The need to push people away.

The deep-down belief that if anyone saw what was inside you,
they would not love you.

The awful belief that you cannot trust yourself
to know how you truly feel.

So much energy gets spent in trying not to remember that you can never feel at peace with yourself. I so get it … I've been there with you.

The greatest gift I got by remembering and in my abuse recovery was learning to trust myself. To truly know what I believe and feel and not be afraid to voice it. I allowed things to happen in my adult life because I didn't feel entitled to speak up.

I learned that it is impossible to believe in yourself when you don't know your own truth. And I learned that when abuse occurs, the abused person learns to dissociate from his or her body where feelings are felt.

We abused people tell ourselves that what is happening isn't really happening or some other lie to keep ourselves removed. Protected.

Because of my ability to deny my truth, I couldn't trust the way I felt. I would go back and forth in my head, which led to confusion and my belief that I was crazy. For years, I felt that way. I learned to lie to myself as you may have. That I was at fault as if this little girl chose to be in the situation I was in. As you may have been in.

Children are easy to manipulate, especially when they are looking for love, attention, and acceptance. And abusing adults know that they can be the puppeteer. Understand that when an older person is in control, it isn't a choice for a child. Me ... and you. It isn't a choice when you are raped. It isn't a choice, even as an adult, until you free yourself from the bondage of abuse.

These are the gifts I have gotten from walking through my abuse: the awareness of it, and the recovery from it. I love feeling free; feeling courageous; sleeping without fear; no longer afraid of the dark and free from nightmares; feeling whole and having self-respect; trusting myself in all situations; asking for what I need; knowing how to keep myself safe; refusing to live in fear; being free to love and feel my sexuality; feeling alive and present; loving myself and the Little Lori that had to live in the abuse; knowing what is okay and not okay for me; being free of self-doubt and self-criticism; being free from self-destructive behaviors; feeling empowered; and my willingness to go to any lengths on my behalf. This is the new me ... and it can be you as well.

Remember ... it is essential to hear, to understand, and to believe:

Dirty and shameful things
were done to me
by a dirty and shameful perpetrator.
I was not protected
because of others' denial.
It does not mean I am not worthy.

The road to recovery is hard, painful, and scary. And at times, it can feel that it will never get better. Facing all the devastating effects can feel endless, but I am living proof that there is light at the end of a very dark tunnel. If I did not do this recovery, my life would be filled with endless suffering, and I would not have my son.

I have found peace and feel proud of my strength. What I was forced to endure has made me who I am today, and for this I am grateful.

With love from one survivor to another,

LORI

Acknowledgments

My recovery started in 1987. At that time, Survivors of Incest Anonymous, Narcotics Anonymous and Food Addicts Anonymous, twelve step programs, were instrumental in my recovery then and to this day.

Thank you to countless people I sought help from the years of 1987 through 1994: therapists, psychiatrists, personal trainers, bio feedback experts, inpatient programs, AMAC, physical therapists, to my art and music teachers as well as The Empty Cradle for helping to heal my soul.

My survivor friends who I spent a lot of time with particularly Judith and Madelyn. Although Judith passed away many years ago, Madelyn continues to be my survivor buddy and a loving, supportive friend. As well as Jamie, my New York friend, for many years. I am grateful to Madelyn and Jamie who believe in me and are a testament to my growth over the years.

And to all the survivors who paved the way for me to heal.

I am grateful to John, who helped me feel safe enough to begin my healing journey from incest.

A special thanks to my sister Karen, my brother-in-law Tom, my brother Peter, my niece Tami and my nephew, Michael who encouraged me to tell my story in any way I needed to tell it. They are my family members who I can be completely honest with about incest and the effects it has had in my life. There are no secrets.

I will always be grateful to Jeff, my soul mate, who helped me to see all that I had become. For his music, his friendship, his humor, his playfulness and special attention to my son, Jason.

To my guard dog FoPo, who was my protector during the most terrifying time in my recovery from incest.

To my clients who share their abuse and trauma stories with me. I value being a part of their recovery and grateful that I get to do this work.

And special thanks to Judith Briles, The Book Shepherd, *TheBookShepherd.com* who helped me write my book. I am grateful for her loving support, her wisdom, and her ability to teach. And who will continue to be my mentor and guide. And to her team of people: Rebecca Finkel, who created the cover and interior designs, *FPGD.com*; Kelly Johnson of *CornerstoneVA. com*, better known as Geek Girl; Michelle Renee, website designer, *StreamlineYourBiz.net*; Ashlee Bratton, who creates magic with her eyes and camera, *Ashography.com*; and to Judith's external editors Peggie Ireland and Barb Wilson.

About the Author

Lori Golden is passionate about helping both trauma and abuse survivors on their healing journey. Her work today is an outgrowth of her recovery from childhood incest and addictions.

She has worked in the mental health profession since the seventies, earning her Master's in Social Work from Hunter College in New York with later training at the Gestalt Institute. Eventually, she opened her own private practice. As a Licensed Clinical Social Worker, her practice is a combination of various therapies she has gained knowledge and experience in over the years. She does not limit herself to one modality of practice since her client's needs vary. Lori believes there are many roads that lead to an individual's healing.

In her private practice, she works with individuals, couples and families in and out of recovery from drugs, alcohol, food, co-dependency, sex and love addiction as well as people who suffer from Post Traumatic Stress Disorder resulting from trauma and abuse. A special group of trauma survivors centers on her work with burn survivors and care givers.

Her first book, *My House of Lies,* is a memoir about her addiction, recovery and overcoming childhood incest after thirty-seven years of amnesia. More significantly, the book is her remarkable journey to seek the truth, reclaim parts of herself that was lost to dissociation and addiction, and turn her own trauma and abuse into a passion to help others face their challenges. Lori inspires and motivates others to seek their truth and heal in her consulting and presentations.

Lori Golden's love of the outdoors, water, warm weather, scuba diving and boating moved her from New York to San Diego where she resides.

www.LoriGoldenAuthor.com

How to Work with Lori Golden

If you don't believe your own story within your life, then what becomes true? THE LIES! The result is that victims begin to think, *I must be crazy.*

Lori Golden knows you are not.

One-On-One Consulting

As a specialist in sexual assault, repressed memories, disassociation, and additions, Lori works with a variety of individual through their recovery. It's not uncommon for sexual assault victims to believe that their pain will never end. Lori believes, and lives, that it well. Healing is possible. With willingness and work.

Speaking

Lori shares her journey of recovery from 11 years of incest— from age of 5 to 16. A recovery that took her through multiple addictions including: drugs, promiscuity, relationships, food, even work. Her awakening began when she admitted she was a drug addict. For a seven-year period, through therapies, counseling, and hospitalization, her ugly childhood was revealed.

Through Lori's speeches and retreats, she knows that her words make a difference. They create a wake-up call for those who discount the damage that sexual abuse creates. And, they have become the bridge for so many who thought that they were alone. That life, and they, were hopeless.

> *Lori's calm presence and keen perception of one's struggles is a gift that not all therapist's carry. She has an in-depth understanding of life's challenges and possess tools to sooth and remedy. Lori not only has the ability to steer you to a better place on your path but is willing to dig deep with you and for you in nearly all arenas.*
> **—Lesia S. Cartelli,** Founder/CEO Angel Faces,
> Author, Heart of Fire

To Connect with Lori
for a One-On-One Consult
or check on Speaking Availability,
call or email her at:

(858) 215-2326

LoriGoldenAuthor@gmail.com

Visit her website and subscribe to her blogs.
Connect with Lori on her social media.

www.LoriGoldenAuthor.com

 facebook.com/MyHouseofLies/

 twitter.com/LoriGoldenLCSW

 linkedin.com/in/lori-golden

 instagram.com/lorigoldenlcsw/